A YEAR TO

Enlightenment

365 Steps to Enriching and Living Your Life

E. Raymond Rock

New Page Books
A Division of The Career Press, Inc.
Franklin Lakes, NJ

A YEAR TO ENLIGHTENMENT
EDITED AND TYPESET BY GINA TALUCCI
Cover design by Conker Tree
Printed in the U.S.A. by Book-mart Press

To order this title, please call toll-free 1-800-CAREER-1 (NJ and Canada: 201-848-0310) to order using VISA or MasterCard, or for further information on books from Career Press.

The Career Press, Inc., 3 Tice Road, PO Box 687,
Franklin Lakes, NJ 07417
www.careerpress.com
www.newpagebooks.com

Library of Congress Cataloging-in-Publication Data

Rock, E. Raymond, 1941-
    A year to enlightenment : 365 steps to enriching and living your life / by E. Raymond Rock.
        p. cm.
    Includes bibliographical references and index.
    ISBN-13: 978-1-56414-891-9
    ISBN-10: 1-56414-891-2
        1. Meditation. 2. Meditations. I. Title.

BL627.R617 2006
204′.32--dc22

                                                                    2006012353

Dedication and Acknowledgments

To Janet, who has been with me every step of the way. You held unwaveringly true to our solitary wedding vow, "To help each other find Truth in this lifetime." Your life reflects the deepest meaning of true friendship.

Bhante Henepola Gunaratana (Bhante "G"), who teaches what he is: love. And Bhante Rahula, welcoming all to the Bhavana Society with loving kindness and compassion.

The beloved Ajahn Chah, who gave me these words to ponder just as the illness that would take his life began: "You can't find a diamond in a rock."

The late Roshi Kennett, who encouraged me to "Go Beyond."

Ajahn Maha Boowa, whose wisdom reminded me to look closely at my arrogance; and Tan Dick and the late Ajahn Pannavaddho, who helped and encouraged me to ordain.

Ajahn Lee and Ajahn Luen, who gave Janet the rare opportunity to live secluded in the forest as a Buddhist nun and meditate night and day on her little bamboo platform.

Ajahn Sumedho, the American monk with the big heart who always took Janet and me, "The Rocks from Boulder," in without question.

Ajahn Passano and Ajahn Amaro who helped us through the difficult beginnings in Thailand and the UK.

Ajahn Brahmavamso, mentoring me long distance by post from Australia about jhanas while I was living in Thailand.

Sueng Sahn Sunim, whose words still haunt me: "Don't know! Don't know! Don't you understand, stupid?"

Trungpa Rinpoche, teaching me what an enlightened being actually is, thus destroying my ideas of what one should be.

Roshi Kozan, who married Janet and I, and Roshi Koshin, who welcomed us to help begin construction of his monastery in McKenna, Washington.

Jack Kornfield and his book, "Living Buddhist Masters," which initially encouraged us to train in Thailand.

The Zen Center in San Franciso where I learned so much about myself.

Jeff Olson of the Velocity Agency, my agent, publishing mentor, and good friend who believed in my book and wouldn't quit.

The hard working people at Career Press/New Page Books: Ron Fry and Michael Pye who made this all possible, Adam Schwartz, Kristen Parkes, Jeff Piasky, Kirsten Dalley, Gina Talucci (my creative editor and ally with boundless patience), Linda Rienecker, Allison Olson, and all the wonderful behind-the-scenes people that an author never has an opportunity to personally thank.

Geoff Huggins, who has always supported my efforts in so many ways.

All who took us under their wings at those precious times when Janet and I were almost penniless and destitute during this amazing journey: Patty, Hugh, Valerie, and Justine; the late Dolores, Jimmy, Danny, and Karen; David, Juanita, Davita, and Chako; Donny, Virginia, Ann, Carrie, and Iris; Aunt Ann and Uncle Jack; Aunt Helen; Rob Drew, Frances Taylor, and Warren Rovetch.

And especially, to Beth and Jerry, Scott, Shellie, and Neil.

My heartfelt thanks to all of you.

Contents

Introduction

People of all beliefs, religions, and perspectives are beginning to ask profound questions: Why are we here? Where did we come from? Where are we going? What are we? Could it be that the answers to our questions are hidden in books somewhere that we haven't yet discovered, or are they simply locked up deep in our own hearts, patiently awaiting discovery?

But how do we unlock our hearts? Can ordinary people such as you and I even consider an unbelievable transformation of consciousness, a remarkable change in values so that we act from our true center at all times? Is it possible to comprehend the unimaginable depths of our being and come face-to-face with the Source of all understanding? Can we free ourselves from conflict; can we become enlightened?

Sometimes we find answers through powerful experiences that dramatically change our lives. People recover from traumatic events or serious illnesses, for example, and become mystically transformed, as if they have been dropped into another lifetime, into another existence in which their previous fear-driven, day-to-day struggles disappear in the wake of an incredible, liberating calmness. The unfounded and exaggerated fears that dominated their "previous lifetimes" now vanish, replaced by inexplicable feelings of purpose and love.

But we needn't wait for traumatic events to improve our lives; we can choose, whenever we wish, to embark upon the ultimate pursuit and the deepest of human experiences, that mysterious state of mind coveted by truth seekers throughout history—spiritual enlightenment. But how do we work toward it and how will it change us?

Indeed, why should we pursue enlightenment at all? And what are the qualifications for beginning this extraordinary quest? More importantly, where will we find a teacher?

A Year to Enlightenment helps you uncover answers to these questions and more in its gently profound, innovative, and clear style, designed to awaken your being to not only the beauty and love all around you, but to the beauty and love you inherently are. Within these mystical pages, you will not only explore your own inner world, but owing to the book's very distinctive, interactive quality, you will have an opportunity to understand in your heart what spiritual enlightenment is all about. Instead of merely reading about enlightenment, you will find yourself actually working toward it.

The Teacher Is... You

Unfortunately, there are no examinations to determine the depth of a spiritual teacher's understanding, but if such a test existed, would it measure knowledge or insight? And who has the credentials to judge such a thing? Do we fall in love by studying about love, or does love happen when we are open and vulnerable? Who, then, is qualified to teach?

The one qualified to teach must ultimately be you, the reader, for who else can prove things true to his or her own intuitive heart? Who else would you believe? Teachers can point the way by offering authentic road maps of the hills and valleys they have trekked, they can indicate points of interest and hazards, but you are the one who now must travel if you want to see and touch the wonders of the landscape for yourself. Therefore, A Year to Enlightenment encourages you to develop your own insight and wisdom. If you read the book to accumulate knowledge, as you have read books in the past, this is all that you will achieve—knowledge—which is merely the map. The answers you are seeking lie beyond mundane knowledge in the realms of transcendent insight and wisdom, and because insight and wisdom can never be learned, only experienced, welcome to a unique journey.

The only requirement to find unconditional understanding and love is resolve. It doesn't take a whiz kid or any letters after one's name to work toward enlightenment; it only requires a thirst for truth. You can do it yourself, regardless of your past. Christ received his education in the sparse desert, and the Buddha in a lonely forest. Solitude was their core curriculum. Only their direct experience of the Source of Understanding within instilled the insight and wisdom required to teach others about the many subtle facets in this journey toward Truth, and to ultimately change the world.

Take Your Time

A Year to Enlightenment was written for brave hearts prepared to embark on an incredible journey. By diving into the waters of spirituality, you have an opportunity to replace your underlying fear and uncertainty with confidence and love. You will find yourself bathed in expansive and universal insights, with each day of the book disclosing a unique, timeless wisdom known by few. This, in turn, surreptitiously opens new, unexplored regions of life and true freedom. If you conscientiously follow the instructions in this comprehensive guide, expect that enlightenment will not be beyond your reach.

But we tangle our lives in many ways, and untangling snarled fishing line requires gentleness and patience. The first knots are extremely tight and if we pull too hard they only become worse, so don't hurry. And don't quit when the road gets rough; be a warrior. Change course this time and take a different approach; work with this book one day at a time, slowly, carefully, completely; savoring it like fine wine—and taste something you have never, in your wildest dreams, thought possible.

For more information and links for this book, go on the Web and visit *www.ayeartoenlightenment.com.*

How to Use This Book

Each of the 365 days in this book brings you closer to spiritual enlightenment through meditation and personal insights. No previous experience with meditation is necessary. *A Year to Enlightenment* will show you how to meditate step-by-step as you travel an amazing road toward an enlightenment that is ultimately indefinable, yet arguably the most important thing you can do for yourself and all other beings.

Three penetrating areas: a daily Insight, a daily Reflection, and a daily Meditation come alive each day. This blending alone is unique, but now imagine each day building on the last, when simple attention moves into powerful stages of concentration, energy-center development, mindfulness, insight, and ultimately into the profound worlds of no-self and emptiness where unconditional love is born.

Reading each day carefully, and working with not more than one day in a 24 hour period is required. This will be a different experience from reading a book in perhaps a few sittings. Personal intuitive indicators signify when it is time for you to move from day to day. These indicators are unique; they are experiential, based upon your individual insights rather than intellectual accumulations of facts. Using your own intuition in this manner allows you to proceed at your own pace, while at the same time proving to you that meaningful steps are being made toward spiritual enlightenment.

Work patiently, one day at a time until you experience an insight either during sitting meditation or while out and about in daily activites. These new insights are what change destinies, but because the nature of each new insight depends on the accumulated experiences of the insights preceding it, don't skip ahead in the book; it's important to work with each day in succession.

Awakenings can happen in colossal ways, or seemingly insignificant ways—perhaps nothing more than becoming aware of another being's deep pain, or noticing that solitary tree you have passed a million times and never really seen. Or maybe such a simple thing as experiencing a subtle change in yourself.

At the bottom of each page, you will find a Journal section where you will record the date and details of the particular insight you experienced while working with that particular day. This will become a record of your personal spiritual journey.

If you are weary of superficial spirituality and thirst for something more meaningful, be prepared to go deeper. This requires patience and working seriously and diligently with only one day at a time as if that particular day was the only day in the book, and then making certain that you experience a new insight, either during meditation or in your daily activities, before moving on to the next day. Insights might not occur daily. You might find yourself remaining on a particular page for many days, or even weeks.

These insightful experiences become your teachers, signaling you to move forward to the next day. You may be tempted to race through the book, because it reflects life from fascinating perspectives, but simply reading it quickly without experiencing these things for yourself will change nothing, and what will you then do with the rest of your life?

Has a persistent rush to accomplishment and thirst for knowledge reduced your stress or improved your relationships? Perhaps when you slow down and touch your heart, instead of only your head, things will change, deep inside, for each insight revealed will alter your life, your destiny, and perhaps the world.

Medical Disclaimer

Meditation is generally safe. There have been a small number of reports that intensive meditation could cause or worsen symptoms in people who have certain psychiatric problems, but this question has not been fully researched. Individuals who are aware of an underlying psychiatric disorder and want to start meditation should speak with a mental health professional before doing so. (Source: BACKGROUNDER: Meditation for Health Purposes, *http://nccam.nih.gov/health/meditation/* May 25, 2006).

Part I: Concentration
Stage 1: Applied and Sustained Attention

Concentration practice creates permanent shifts in consciousness. After a shift takes place, everything is seen in a different light. Depending on the strength of the shift, this new vision could be subtle, astonishing, or anything in between.

Part Two of this book involves mindfulness, which subjectively directs the concentrated mind to investigate specific objects within our bodies and minds. This combination of investigating specialized objects with a deepening consciousness creates wisdom and insight.

Part Three involves understanding the roots of our illusions; a "doer" and "doing," and therefore leads to release.

The process of enlightenment flows, with no real starting point or steps; however, you must work with what you are now, not with what you perceive yourself to be or what you plan to be. Each day of practice, each shift in consciousness, refines your awareness of what you actually are. In the beginning, you might fight with all your heart until your heart finds its release. If you attempt to release yourself through little effort, realization will be next to impossible. Review the How to Use This Book section, and follow the instructions carefully.

Be a beginner at all times, even though you might not consider yourself a beginner. Start fresh and do each meditation lesson completely and as perfectly as you can. Try not to bring opinions along with you. If you think the initial steps are too easy, then determine to do them perfectly. This will challenge you until you are gradually introduced to deeper meditation procedures. The simple, day-by-day instructions are designed not to overwhelm you. You will be able to keep up easily with the process while making solid improvements in every facet of your life.

Insights, as described, will occur when you penetrate into a truth bypassing old conditioning. They're a breath of fresh air that changes you, and even if they are seemingly insignificant insights, once they occur you will never return to exactly what or who you were. You will become aware of kind acts, as well as disingenuous acts. You will notice how you feel in a forest—and the feeling of walls. You might see your striving, doubting, or escaping, perhaps your bravery or cowardice. You might find yourself in ecstasy or wandering about in long, dark periods when all hope is gone. As your concentration deepens, your awareness of insights will sharpen, and then the insights themselves will deepen to new levels as your consciousness shifts. Keep your awareness antennae up at all times, because everything observed will be new.

DAY 1

Insight

A meadow of delicate, spring flowers. Hopeful faces turned toward the sun.

Reflections

Many books were there to choose from, but for some reason, I chose this one. Was it curiosity, or is something guiding me toward...something? I feel as if I'm trying to find my way home after being gone for such a long time, but so far, books have only been roadmaps for me. I'll actually have to take that first, tentative step if my journey is to begin.

Meditation

True meditation is difficult to define. It happens when you forget yourself. You can't achieve it in the same way you soak up knowledge, because your desire to master meditation is exactly what prevents you from experiencing it. It is a riddle. For now, lay down and just close your eyes and picture your favorite surroundings. That could include lying on a sun-drenched beach, walking through damp, pungent forests, or maybe gazing at the blue mountain skies of winter— wherever you feel relaxed and comfortable. Remain there as you take a deep breath, and when you let it out, relax your shoulders and face by letting them fall along with your out breath. Now breathe naturally and remain completely at ease for about 10 minutes, imagining yourself in your favorite place. Keep all random thoughts away for now. As a reminder, remember to remain on this page until a new experience or insight arises. A new insight or experience can be as simple as noticing how your mind jumps around when you try to visualize your special place.

Personal Journal

_____

_____

_____

_____ *Date* _____

A Year to Enlightenment

DAY 2

Insight

Just one moment in time.

Reflections

A solitary butterfly resting on a leaf with wings folded—so motionless. Is this a symbol of the hushed, natural world of all beings? In this silence, will I find that which I can only now long for?

Meditation

Close your eyes and feel your body breathing, then imagine yourself in your favorite surroundings again. Just notice your breathing as you rest there, keeping other thoughts away for now. Continue this for about 10 minutes. Try to meditate twice a day, preferably when you first awaken and just before bedtime. Remember, don't turn the page until a new insight or experience occurs, regardless of how many days that takes. Then record your insights below in your personal journal.

Personal Journal

_____

_____

_____

_____ Date _____

DAY 3

Insight

A clear stream, not a rushing current.

Reflections

If only I could move like a brook, wandering along ever-changing woodland scenery, flowing relaxed and ever watchful.

Meditation

Your meditation sessions will begin with a simple breathing exercise as follows: Take a deep inhalation for about five seconds, filling your lungs. Begin this inhalation from the tip of your tailbone and visualize it as a ball of intense white light moving, in a seemingly reverse fashion, up your spine and over the top of your head. Then exhale slowly for about 10 seconds, imagining the light showering over your chest and between your legs like a waterfall, releasing all of the tensions in your body as they fall along with it. Repeat this cycle three times around the back and down the chest and then remain bathed in your shower of white light as your breath floods and cleanses your entire body. Spend the remaining 10 minutes imagining your favorite place again and relaxing there. Don't allow stray thoughts to distract you. Allow them to pass through.

Personal Journal

_____

_____

_____

_____ Date _____

DAY 4

Insight

The truth, like a spotless lens, is many times looked past.

Reflections

Soft petals of wildflowers touching my cheek. A snowflake melting on my tongue. Childhood memories? Are they really so childish? How close to the truth?

Meditation

Begin with your three circling breaths of white light. Similar to learning to play a flute, there will be some clumsiness at first, but soon you will be running the breath around your body with ease! This exercise, when done properly and daily, may have the power to cure and prevent physical diseases. Practice meditation every day, at the same time of day, if possible. Set aside a separate practice area, perhaps with a candle and some flowers, to help move your mind away from worldly concerns for these special 10 minutes. After your opening exercise today, return to that favorite place in your mind where you can relax. Try to practice twice a day if possible, and at the same time. If thoughts get in the way, remember that it's normal for the mind to think. If you watch thoughts carefully with an overvie w and without becoming involved with them, they will pass through on their own, and you will soon discover their transient nature. Don't forget; don't move ahead until an insight is experienced and recorded in your journal.

Personal Journal 🪷

_____
_____ _____
_____
_____ _Date_ _____

DAY 5

Insight

I sit quietly, watching my snow castles of knowledge melt beneath the sun.

Reflections

I'll have to be quick to catch a glimpse of truth. It is so fast!

Meditation

Begin with your warm-up exercise. Then draw the next breath of white light into your solar plexus, just above your navel. Exhale slowly, completely, maintaining your concentration of the white light in your solar plexus. The exhalation should be two or three times longer than the inhalation. For example, if you breathe in for 2 seconds, breathe out for 4 to 6 seconds. Allow the body to take the in breath on its own, naturally, and then purposely extend the exhalation. Focus on your solar plexus, or the point of your diaphragm that rises and falls, just above your navel. Resist breathing high in your chest, as this causes stress, keep your breathing in the solar plexus area. Be aware of your breath at all times as it cleanses your body, but don't follow it up and down or in and out. The breath should always be flooding your body in the background, with your main focus at your diaphragm. The solar plexus is your object of concentration now. Practice this breathing rhythm during your 15-minute meditation sessions today. Concentrating on your diaphragm will be your primary focus, but be aware of each inhalation and each exhalation as well, long or short, restricted or free, but keep them in the background.

Personal Journal

_____

_____

_____

_____ Date _____

A Year to Enlightenment

DAY 6

Insight

Nature is closer.

Reflections

I love to stroll through a quiet forest, gaze at the magnificent mountains, and relax in the warm waters of the tranquil ocean. I feel their vastness, their majesty, their full emptiness. Are they guiding me toward that infinite, eternal essence within?

Meditation

Sit on the floor on a pad or carpet. Cross your legs Indian style and place a small, firm pillow under the tip of your tailbone. You may sit on the edge of a chair in an erect position or lie down, for modified positions. Silence is best, but if you live in a noisy household, mask the commotion with headphones. It is better to avoid music during meditation, but recordings of soothing nature sounds are okay. Don't forget the three preliminary circling breaths. You will follow the breaths in the form of a ball of white light around your body, but when you are concentrating on your meditation object, which in this case is your solar plexus, do not follow the breaths in and out or up and down. Your primary focus will be a point in the solar plexus. Watch your body draw natural incoming breaths into your solar plexus, and then purposely extend the outgoing breath two or three times longer. Don't forget to keep your primary attention and the ball of white light in the solar plexus, with only a background focus on your breath. If the focus of attention and light seem to drift away from the solar plexus, don't disturb your concentration by repositioning them into your solar plexus; allow them to remain where they are. Remain focused on the light no matter where it travels. Sit for 15 minutes during each session.

Personal Journal

_____

_____

_____

_____ Date _____

DAY 7

Insight

Security and creativity never mix, just like oil and water, like fear and love.

Reflections

I remember falling in love for the first time. I had always imagined what it would be like, but the reality of it left my feeble expectations awash in its powerful wake.

Meditation

Don't forget: Begin with three deep breaths, bringing them up your back in the form of a white ball of light, around the top of your head, and down your chest in a circle. Spend 4 or 5 seconds inhaling up the back, and 8 to 12 seconds exhaling down over the chest and between the legs, before the breath starts back up the spine again. Next, breathe into the solar plexus, with the length of the inhale and exhale being a ratio of 1 to 2 or 1 to 3. Your strength and concentration increase during the out breath, and this is why it is prolonged. If you are sitting cross-legged on the floor, tuck your left heel between your legs and try to place your right ankle on top of your left thigh, on top of your left calf, or on the floor next to your left calf while keeping both knees firmly on the floor. This might take some getting used to. When using a chair, sit on the edge with your feet flat on the ground and your back straight. If, for physical reasons, it's difficult to maintain either of these positions, then any motionless posture is okay. Now, for today's sessions, try to maintain your sitting position for 20 minutes. In the background, keep that feeling of your first, powerful love in mind—just the feeling, not the memories.

Personal Journal

_____
_____
_____
_____ Date _____

A Year to Enlightenment

DAY 8

Insight

The threshold; emptiness.

Reflections

I once lost someone who was close. Do you know how I felt? I felt tremendously empty.

Meditation

While meditating, your hands should be relaxed, lying in your lap, palms up, one cupped within the other. Your left hand should be underneath, with the right hand on top, and your thumb tips touching very lightly. An alternative position of the thumbs, which increases the power of concentration for some people, is to make a circle with your thumb and index finger of each hand, then as you cup your hands, join these two circles so it makes a "OO" formation with opposite index fingers and thumbs touching. After your three circling breaths today, concentrate on breathing into your solar plexus and maintaining the position of your hands and fingers. In the background, keep the feeling of emptiness or loss in your heart. Sit for 20 minutes during your sessions until you get to day 15.

Personal Journal

_____
_____
_____
_____ Date _____

DAY 9

Insight

Only when escape is no longer necessary, do we fully escape.

Reflections

When I feel empty, it really does frighten me. I have no choice but to run from it. How can I relieve the uncomfortable feeling? How can I fill this emptiness?

Meditation

Make certain that your spine doesn't slump during meditation—this is essential to productive meditation. Retain the natural inward curve of your spine in the small of your back by thrusting your hips foreword. Never allow yourself to slump in this area. Remember to begin each session with your three circling breaths, and then concentrate on both your breathing into the solar plexus and your posture. Try to know every in breath and out breath as it fills your body with healing energy. Your hands should be in the correct position and your back should be curved naturally inward. Your shoulders and legs should be relaxed, feeling only a slight tension to keep the back curved inwardly. In time, as you learn to thrust your hips forward, this tension will relax as well. Keep the feeling of emptiness in your heart again today, but keep it in the background.

Personal Journal

_____

_____

_____

_____ Date _____

DAY 10

Insight

The sage with laughing eyes said, "Unlike you, I have nothing left to lose!"

Reflections

Now I know what fills my caverns of emptiness; I create treasures.

Meditation

The position of your neck is very important. It should not be tilted forward or backward, but upright and stretched toward the sky while at the same time your arms should be relaxed and fall from your shoulders. Relax your face and eyes as well. Your chin should be tucked in slightly. For today's session, begin with your three circling breaths. After that, draw the incoming breaths into your solar plexus, as instructed, and then completely exhaust the outgoing breaths. Your out breath should be two or three times as long as the in breath. Sit upright, with the small of your back curved naturally inward, thrusting your hips forward to maintain this position. Keep your head upright, not tilting forward or backward, and stretch your neck upward, tucking your chin in slightly. It is important that you remain relaxed at all times and not become tense. If you feel tense, relax for a few moments and breathe normally and deeply, then continue your practice. Spend your entire session monitoring your posture, your solar plexus, and breathing, and make certain that you remain relaxed. Thoughts that come and go should be allowed to pass through; don't become stuck on them.

Personal Journal

_____
_____
_____
_____ Date _____

DAY 11

Insight

Knot upon knot, entanglements grow.

Reflections

Is there some tiny part of my busy world that I can simplify? I've spent considerable time and energy filling up my life, haven't I? Maybe it's time to make a little space.

Meditation

You may keep your eyes open or closed, as you prefer. If open, keep them only half or barely open, gazing at the floor 3 or 4 feet in front of you. Try not to glance around. When using a chair, your feet should be able to touch the floor and your thighs should be parallel so that your knees are neither higher nor lower than your hips. If you are sitting on the floor, some back discomfort or knee ache can be expected until your body adjusts to the posture. Don't be too quick to surrender to pain or numbness or you won't learn about them. On the other hand, always treat yourself kindly regarding acute pain at this stage in your practice. If the pain doesn't subside after a reasonable amount of time, adjust your position. Later, you will be able to disassociate the pain from the body, and neither the pain nor the fear will be a problem. Today's meditation assignment will be to monitor your posture, your meditation object, and your breathing. Also be sure to notice the cycles of pain that might arise in your back or legs, and how the pain affects you mentally.

Personal Journal

_____
_____
_____
_____ Date _____

DAY 12

Insight

Destinations reveal paths traveled.

Reflections

Am I going to invest an entire lifetime accomplishing worldly dreams and ambitions? Perhaps I'd better consider the results. Many times in the past, I've confused myself regarding concept and reality.

Meditation

If possible, breathe through your nose during meditation, and relax. Everything should be relaxed, peaceful, and still, with your body as motionless as possible. Moving around, swallowing, sniffing, scratching, clearing your throat, and so forth are considered hindrances, and hindrances can be extremely clever. You might think your valuables (your vulnerabilities and weaknesses) are put away in a safe, but the hindrances somehow know the combinations to your safes, and will steal you blind without you noticing. Hindrances make you lazy, sleepy, listless, irritable, numb, distracted, and will create a lack of confidence. "I just can't do this, this isn't me." "Is my effort worth it?" "Maybe I'll try this again later, when I'm not so busy." Hindrances will create concerns about alienating friends and relatives, or persuade you to seek intellectual answers to spiritual questions. Today, see how long you can monitor your posture, solar plexus, and breathing before stray thoughts or hindrances steal your attention. If they do, discover them quickly and gently refocus your attention to your breathing and posture.

Personal Journal

_____
_____
_____
_____ Date _____

DAY 13

Insight

Body and mind—no difference!

Reflections

When I'm happy, I'm energized, and when I'm in peak physical condition, my attitude is great! Are my body and mind connected? What's beyond them both?

Meditation

Your whole body should be stress-free with only your back muscles or legs feeling some pressure, along with a slight tension in keeping your neck stretched upward and your chin slightly tucked in. The rest of your body, including your stomach, should be relaxed. If you can swivel your hips far enough forward, even the muscular stress holding your back straight will relax as your entire body settles into a state of perfect ease and balance without effort. After your three circling breaths today, continue monitoring your posture, meditation object, and breathing—and keep track of whether or not you feel relaxed, particularly in your shoulders. The most difficult time for new meditators is at the beginning, after the amusement of a new pastime wears off and nothing particularly exciting is happening. It requires perseverence at this point. Most worthwhile things in life take time, so remain patient, and trust your guide.

Personal Journal

_____

_____

_____

_____ Date _____

DAY 14

Insight

Seek inwardly.

Reflections

I've heard every belief imaginable regarding the next world. A friend of mine claims that we are nothing, that we are merely accidents of nature, and when we die, we'll simply fall into a dreamless sleep—for eternity! I can't even imagine eternity! Others say that we will remain who we are, but in a heavenly realm—that sounds nice. Some say that we come back to Earth many times in different forms to live life over and get it right. But how will I know for sure what is true? Is it possible to know this without having to die first? How would I do that?

Meditation

Today, monitor your posture, solar plexus, and your breathing as usual, but in the background, bring up a feeling of joy. Wrap it around the whole world. Don't allow your everyday thoughts to interfere or let your opinions get in the way. Generate this feeling of joy outward toward the entire world during both sessions today. Don't forget to remain on this day until an insight is experienced, then record it in your journal at the bottom of the page.

Personal Journal

_____

_____

_____

_____ Date _____

DAY 15

Insight

What moves mountains?

Reflections

If my actions on Earth affect my destiny in some future world, how should I act? If I follow rules outwardly, will that really change me inwardly? What part of me changes—the same part that moves on? What is it that worries about these things anyway?

Meditation

If you can arrange it, a separate room for meditation is supportive. It should be quiet, cool, and subdued with the curtains drawn. Loose fitting, light clothing is best to keep your legs unrestricted and your body cool, which tends to heat up during meditation. Increase your practice to 25 minutes today, and during your sessions, as a background to your posture, solar plexus, and breathing awareness, imagine yourself happy. Spread that feeling to everybody you know, especially the ones you dislike! If you think the present meditation period is too long or too short, try to see this as merely an opinion, a thought, and watch it arise and fleetingly disappear, making way for the next opinion that soon will follow.

Personal Journal

_____

_____

_____

_____ Date _____

DAY 16

Insight

Your secret key is deep inside.

Reflections

I can imagine a secret key that opens a treasure chest of light, freeing humankind from all the conflict, sorrow, and discontent that has prevailed since the beginning of time. I ponder the cost of such a priceless key. Perhaps everything?

Meditation

Feel a sense of humility today as a background to your posture, solar plexus, and breathing practice. Believe for a moment that you are no better or worse than whomever you meet on the street, regardless who that person might be. Keep this feeling in your heart for each of your 25-minute sessions today.

Personal Journal

_____

_____

_____

_____ Date _____

DAY 17

Insight

Know not your brothers and sisters, but yourself.

Reflections

I could study many things, but if I only studied one, myself, until I knew the truth about it, how far would this carry me?

Meditation

Extend your practice to 30-minute sessions now. As a background to your breathing, your meditation object, and your posture, bring up a feeling of loving kindness. Keep this feeling in your heart and spread it among all beings in the far corners of the worlds. Never worry about personal achievements in meditation. Instead, remain in the proper posture monitoring your breathing. As you become proficient in posture and breathing, and as they become automatic, stray thoughts will creep in to complicate your practice. These will appear as mental pictures, verbal chatter, or internal conversations. Just observe these thoughts and allow them to dissolve on their own.

Personal Journal

_____

_____

_____

_____ Date _____

DAY 18

Insight

Virtue and Purity—two lions guard the heart door.

Reflections

Is insight like falling in love—something that just happens to us? I probably can't hurry this insight, study it, or achieve it. Maybe insight arrives as an unexpected flash, hitting me so hard that I could never mistake it as not being the truth. Is this what meditation is all about, stilling my mind so that this mystical insight can strike? Where does insight come from and how can I attract it? I'll just bet that insight requires a virtuous mind. I wouldn't be surprised if virtue will be my first priority!

Meditation

During your 30-minute sessions, be attentive and wide-awake. Completely relax with your practice, monitoring your posture, your solar plexus, your breathing, and simply notice the many thoughts that will flit through your mind. Meditation should never be a white-knuckled affair; it should only involve complete, relaxed attention. If you inject tension into your meditation, your body will release the tension by involuntarily jerking or swaying back and forth. This is temporary and will cease as you learn to relax.

Personal Journal

_____
_____
_____
_____ Date _____

DAY 19

Insight

Walk beside virtue.

Reflections

What is keeping me from being virtuous? You know, virtue, those self-effacing qualities of humility, self-sacrifice, compassion, generosity, and restraint that astonish me when I see them. Maybe I'm afraid to be virtuous because this would involve my becoming vulnerable. Is this what I would I be risking if I authentically became virtuous, rather than pretending to be virtuous? How can I end this pretending? Perhaps I should begin by honestly acknowledging my pretenses.

Meditation

Begin, as always, with your three circling breaths, followed by attention to your solar plexus, posture, and breathing. Then, for your 30-minute sessions today, keep the feeling of loving kindness in the background, directing it toward someone you dislike or have disliked in the past. This might feel similar to surrender, or even develop into stubborn refusal, but regardless of your feelings, continually return to loving kindness. It is common for new meditators to experience their legs falling asleep. This is usually caused by sitting too fully on a cushion. It is tempting to sit high up on a large cushion so that your knees are flat on the ground, but circulation is sometimes cut off, resulting in numbness. To correct this, a firm cushion should be placed only at the very tip of the tailbone. The knees will eventually flatten out with additional sitting.

Personal Journal

_____

_____

_____

_____ Date _____

A Year to Enlightenment

DAY 20

Insight

True meditation fills the heart.

Reflections

What can I do? My mind is simply not virtuous. Selfish greed, deceit, and confusion—that's me! I'm full of sensual cravings and always wanting things to go my way. At the same time, I insist that other things do not happen, and if things again don't go my way, I become upset and angry. Then I become confused—who or what is experiencing all of this—my body or my mind? I become completely immersed in my feelings and mental states, and when something delights or disgusts me, I keep recalling the sensation until it becomes a strong emotion, an attachment, and a yoke around my neck. My advancement toward the spiritual life is impossible in this state of mind. I must find a way to cultivate virtue. I want it and I must have it, but how can I attain genuine virtue with this obsessive mind that must get what it wants? I'll surely resort to my old habits such as jealousy and hatred. It is a confusing state of affairs.

Meditation

After finishing your warm-up exercise, monitor your posture and breathing, keeping your primary focus on your solar plexus. Then watch the many thoughts that appear, but don't become involved; observe them until they move along by themselves. Begin introducing your meditation into daily life by finding a quiet place to walk or cycle. Try to keep all thoughts subdued by simply observing and not registering. For example, when you notice a tree, don't label it as a pine tree, or even a tree for that matter, just notice it and go on to the next thing. Begin with a few moments of this and then work toward a bike ride or walk without one thought arising. Keep your sessions to 30 minutes until day 33.

Personal Journal

_____

_____

_____

_____ _Date_ _____

DAY 21

Insight

Those gentle beings, the not-noticed, are sorely missed when gone.

Reflections

Greed and aggressiveness run rampant in my small mind. Can one insignificant, genuinely kind person, full of love, make a difference? Yes, I know that this person can, if I'm ever fortunate enough that we meet. Perhaps it will change my life.

Meditation

Follow your regular routine of the three circling breaths, and then continue watching your posture, your breath, and your thoughts in the background, with your primary focus on your solar plexus. Can you see the thoughts come and go without getting involved? While walking and cycling, try not to verbalize; for example, I must remember to drop by the bank today. Keep your mind as silent as possible and focused on your awareness of the body breathing, with the breath flooding and purifying every part of you. Also, just notice the various things in nature and let them go without dwelling on them. These practices take time to develop, and the benefits will not be immediately apparent. Over time, however, there will be an alteration in your consciousness.

Personal Journal

_____

_____

_____

_____ Date _____

DAY 22

Insight

Profound meditation brings on enlightenment; enlightenment is profound meditation.

Reflections

My life is a series of circles. Each experience builds on the past to create new castles in my sky, with each circling a little higher or lower than the previous one. And as I spiral through this life, seemingly unconscious at times, being shoved here and there as if by invisible forces, I can only speculate what would happen if the circles would somehow be...disrupted.

Meditation

Ideally, you are developing a daily routine. The secret to sharpening a knife is a light stropping every day only to straighten the edge. Waiting until a knife is dull requires a hard grinding, and soon the blade is ruined. Are you remembering the three breaths to begin each session, your breathing, and posture? Review everything to make certain you have not forgotten any points. You will soon be adding an additional beginning exercise, a complex but necessary one to keep your body and mind balanced as your meditation deepens. Today, continue to notice your breathing and posture.

Personal Journal

_____
_____
_____
_____ _Date_ _____

DAY 23

Insight

For only one day, follow your heart completely, without yesterday's or tomorrow's baggage.

Reflections

Meditation and spiritual enlightenment are certainly mysteries. I'm not sure what they are but I know what they are not; they are not shallow escapes to avoid facing life, which is fraught with stress, and they don't involve a group coddling of oneself. They seem to be unique gifts that I am quietly awaiting with a familiar certainty. I know they'll come to me when the time is right, and I know that I will be utterly amazed.

Meditation

Meditate on loving kindness again today as a background to your posture, breathing, and solar plexus concentration. Spread your loving kindness generously among all beings. The more you give away, the more you have—not at all like money! If something occasionally comes up that keeps you from practicing, don't be overly concerned; missing a few days during the year is to be expected. But do notice what interrupted your practice and consider how worthwhile it will prove to be in the long run. Many things can occur in meditation to distract you, such as warmness, saliva accumulating that you feel a compulsion to swallow, itchy feelings, and restlessness. All of these things will take care of themselves as your concentration improves.

Personal Journal

_____

_____

_____

_____ _Date_ _____

A Year to Enlightenment

DAY 24

Insight

Like a shooting star surprising us on a clear winter's night, the end comes quickly.

Reflections

Can I change my destiny? I wonder how much time I have left.

Meditation

Relax your mind as well as your body as you continue to concentrate. A word of caution: Don't concentrate so intently that tension builds in your body or mind. Always make certain that you are relaxed and focused. Don't continue feeding disrupting thought patterns that arise—just gently drop them. As your meditation deepens, your mind will come up with seemingly important things to think about. Be careful of the mind's tricks—you'll have plenty of time to think later. As the length of your meditation periods increase, you might see or hear strange things. Not to worry, the moment you experience something bizarre, simply go back to your posture or breathing concentration, open your eyes, or take a few deep breaths. It will vanish. These things are common occurrences with some people and they aren't important. Actually, they become a problem only if the meditator thinks that they are signs of progress and attempts to repeat them, or worse, begins giving lectures or accumulating disciples! Then they become a nuisance and the correct practice of concentrating on the posture, the solar plexus, and the breathing is soon forgotten.

Personal Journal

_____

_____

_____

_____ _Date_ _____

DAY 25

Insight

Wake up!

Reflections

As I wander from scene to scene, stumbling through this stage play called life, I can only hope that someday the sun's light will dispel the persistent fog that creeps into each hollow and blankets every ridge of my beautiful forest.

Meditation

After your three circling breaths, monitor your posture and breathing as usual while primarily focusing on your solar plexus, but also reflect on the many people who have selflessly helped you throughout life without a thought of repayment. Toward the end of each session today, spread gratitude all over the world. If you feel like crying or laughing during meditation for no apparent reason, understand that this is common. It is quite okay to cry or laugh, or do both at the same time! If you find yourself crying because of sad memories however, remember that memories disturb your concentration. The proper practice is to always return to your concentration of the white light in your solar plexus, your posture, and your breathing, and to gently allow thoughts and memories to pass through as soon as they are noticed.

Personal Journal

_____

_____

_____

_____ Date _____

DAY 26

Insight

Generosity...what freedom!

Reflections

I love helping people, animals, insects, even plants. I do it for no reason other than to ease their discomfort with no thought of personal gratification at all, not even thinking about being a nice person. This helping comes from a quiet, loving place, a place quite different from the noisy one that causes my distress.

Meditation

As a background to your concentration today, recall feelings of true generosity and compassion. Stay with these feelings for your entire sessions. Be with the actual feelings more than the ideas or images of them. We create ideas and images in our minds as security, and security will always prevent us from seeing reality.

Personal Journal

_____

_____

_____

_____ Date _____

DAY 27

Insight

The truly disciplined are, of course, completely undisciplined.

Reflections

Can discipline ever change me fundamentally? I hate rules—they're so confining. Do this, do that—I would rather do as I please, but that doesn't seem to work either because I never change. Maybe true discipline comes from within, where somehow I'm able to see in a new way. Then, instead of an imposition, discipline would perhaps become a natural, effortless way of life, filled with order, intelligence, and spontaneity.

Meditation

Meditation is not a religion, movement, or a quick solution. Meditation is a personal endeavor that takes time to develop, so in the beginning you will be operating on blind faith until results are attained. This is why you establish a firm schedule. When you begin training, your mind is understandably wild and undisciplined, only wanting to practice when it is in the mood. It can always find something more interesting to do than meditate! Your mind would rather be involved with action, or anything other than coming face to face with its own emptiness, so it will desperately attempt to escape. For your sessions today, follow your regular routine, and in the background, challenge your mind by staying with the feeling of emptiness.

Personal Journal

_____

_____

_____

_____ *Date* _____

A Year to Enlightenment

DAY 28

Insight

Striving...so violent.

Reflections

At times, I'm not much of an enterprising person; I would rather lay about the beach all day than get ahead in the world. Other times, I'm incredibly aggressive, letting nothing stand in my way. I really don't know who I am. What a dilemma!

Meditation

A particularly productive time to engage in meditation is during the wee hours of the morning, between 3 a.m. and dawn. This is when it is easier to touch a deeper consciousness. Other fruitful times are at sunrise and sunset, or when first arising in the morning and before retiring at night. Actually, anytime is fine, with the possible exception of that hour or two following meals, when you will most certainly fall asleep unless you walk during meditation. (Walking meditation will be explained later.) Today, follow your normal routine: the three circling breaths in the form of a ball of white light, and monitoring your solar plexus, posture, and breathing.

Personal Journal

_____

_____

_____

_____ Date _____

DAY 29

Insight

A glad heart, a peaceful life.

Reflections

I seem to be changing. It is a strange thing. Loving kindness, compassion, gladness, equanimity—they are all cropping up in subtle ways without warning. Just yesterday, I noticed an old man helping his frail, crippled wife walk slowly down the grocery store aisle. He was so gentle, a lifetime of shared experiences reflected in his patience...and I wept.

Meditation

Regularity in your practice is important because a cycle is developing. Only your schedule and your resolve will sustain your practice when you hit the wall of emptiness and it all closes in on you. Your mind, now restricted from its habitual escapes, must face this dreaded boredom and depression that it has been avoiding these many years. Don't run from these two impostors; challenge them and find out exactly how much power they have over you. During your sessions, follow your regular routine and keep your mind still, within whatever arises.

Personal Journal

_____

_____

_____

_____ Date _____

DAY 30

Insight

Love is a brilliant, many-facetted diamond.

Reflections

How can I describe loving kindness? It appears when I see or recognize the underlying love in others, and only then does my antagonism toward them lessen, but still I can't seem to maintain the loving kindness. Soon, I again become wrapped up in myself.

Meditation

As your practice matures, boredom, depression, and every emotion in fact will have far less of an impact. These feelings will be considered as merely passing occurrences, no different from the transient thoughts that march along in your mind. In time, life itself will be seen as a dream, a series of attempted escapes, with meditation being the reality. If, however, your inclination toward the spiritual life has not yet matured, poor effort could be the result, with meditation proving to be little more than a temporary getaway, a mere whim to be swiftly replaced by the next new and alluring amusement. If this is the case, you must practice, while you can, as if your life depends upon it. For your sessions today, sit peacefully with no agenda. No exercises, no breathing, no posture or solar plexus monitoring, no thoughts. Experience the feeling of just being, and not doing.

Personal Journal

_____

_____

_____

_____ Date _____

DAY 31

Insight

Live in harmony. Cause little pain to others.

Reflections

When am I compassionate? I'm compassionate when I feel. It seems to be connected with relieving suffering, both in others and myself, and involves a willingness to open my eyes and really look. After all, how could I remain aloof after seeing the helplessness of those trapped in their distress and conflicts? Can I see, past my pride, the grief I cause myself? Perhaps. Maybe that's where compassion begins.

Meditation

Meditation is always an opening—so that something new can find its way in. That new "something" is beyond your mind, revealing worlds never imagined. During today's sessions, keep yourself open to exactly what is happening in this precise moment in time—"That Which Is." Don't practice exercises or concentration today. Only see what comes up, let it go, and see what arises next.

Personal Journal

_____

_____

_____

_____ Date _____

DAY 32

Insight

Saddened by laughter, gladdened by grief; the sage lives alone.

Reflections

Gladness requires peculiar insight. Genuine gladness about my rival's success requires the absence of petty jealousy. But how can I go beyond petty jealousy without a clear understanding of how fraught with fear jealousy really is, or understand the uniqueness of gladness, which has the power to cure tedium and aversion? What's odd is that when I see something that's funny, gladness is seldom present in my heart. Now, every time I laugh, I search for the root of my laughter. Is it warm, or is it at times, a subtle condescension?

Meditation

You will return to concentration with the next day's sessions, but for now, forgo any ambitions toward enlightenment. Keep your heart kind and relaxed. Be what you are, not what you want to be or should be. It is okay to be you. Just observe.

Personal Journal

_____

_____

_____

_____ Date _____

DAY 33

Insight

I am afraid no longer, my fortune secure in my heart.

Reflections

Equanimity is an extraordinary word and an extraordinary state—not the cold indifference that I had once imagined. How could it be when it is filled with compassion, gladness, and loving kindness? Yet, it is not sentimental or dripping with emotionalism; it is more mature than that. Its uniqueness is equality—no praise, no blame—whether rich or poor, famous or forgotten, while at the same time assuring me that I must eventually answer to my every action.

Meditation

Extend your practice to 40-minute sessions and maintain this until day 46. These 40 minutes are when your mind relaxes into practice and approaches the threshold of deeper states. Concentrate on your solar plexus, breathing, and posture for your entire sessions, ignoring any visions or epiphanies that come up. Only your concentration is important. Visions and meditation experiences are similar to movies on a screen. We are working toward the screen now—the background, not the movies. Visions many times result from thinking so intensely about something that it seems to appear before you. It will seem very real, many times prompted by strong emotions or religious fervor. If the vision is connected to one's belief, it is usually the result of psychological pressure of some kind. If the vision is foreign and puzzling, then this might indicate something other than a construct of the mind. To be on the safe side, however, it is best to ignore all visions. Visions have led many people astray, and can reinforce that which we believe, being very dramatic, yet not conducive to gaining freedom, as we tend to attach and cling to them.

Personal Journal

_____

_____

_____

_____ Date _____

A Year to Enlightenment

DAY 34

Insight

For every smile, a teardrop.

Reflections

How can I develop the beautiful qualities of loving kindness, compassion, gladness, and equanimity if I still harbor selfish desires? Can I ever acquire enough personal security? Must I constantly fight for what I want, pushing others aside, trying to be first in line and last in loyalty? What is the answer?

Meditation

Begin with your normal routine of three circling breaths, followed by your concentration practice. Also rest your mind within purity and virtue by feeling compassion for every being, for each being suffers greatly in his or her own private way.

Personal Journal

_____

_____

_____

_____ Date _____

DAY 35

Insight

Not too fast, not too slow—steady.

Reflections

I suspiciously analyze everything, and my analysis tells me that this meditation is not going to be easy, especially with my critical mind. I have been lied to many times in my life, and a little cynicism is to be expected. I'm determined to see for myself if, with sustained effort, I will truly find my freedom.

Meditation

Be a turtle, slow and steady. You can't assault heaven as you might attack some other challenge. Ambition will fail every time. Your undying passion for truth, however...this will triumph in the end. Be patient and kind with yourself as you slowly gain confidence in a practice that will never abandon you. For today's sessions, concentrate on your solar plexus, posture, and breathing, but watch your busy mind and its myriad of thoughts as well. Understand that the mind's duty is to think, just as the body's duty is to breathe, but remember that the mind and body, they are not you.

Personal Journal

_____
_____
_____
_____ Date _____

Applied Attention

The first stage of concentration involves applying attention. Here, you will direct your mind to a certain meditation object just as you would direct a hammer toward a bell, striking it. You strike the bell (you strike the object with your mind's attention), it rings for a while (as you maintain undivided attention on the object), and then the bell stops ringing (when you lose your attention and your mind drifts off the object and on to something else). Then you must strike the object again, repeatedly, to reestablish your attention. Your initial focus cannot maintain itself for long before drifting away; this is to be expected. Just keep returning to your meditation object again and again; persistent returning is all that is required at this point. With practice, you will be able to remain with the object of your concentration longer, and this will lead you to the next step—a sustainable focus without losing attention.

You will now be given a new meditation object. This will be your focus during meditation sessions. While deeply concentrating on this object, most of your normal, mental, and physical reactions will be suspended. It is like a vacation for your mind and body. Always remain relaxed and don't concentrate so hard that you become tense. Always remain relaxed—relaxed and focused.

DAY 36

Insight

Climbing mountains of mist.

Reflections

New relationships, different clothes, jobs, cars, houses, towns—holding on, letting go, waiting...for something. I have convinced myself repeatedly that whatever it is I'm waiting for is just over that next mountain, but when I scramble up my mountain and excitedly look over the top for my deliverance, all I see is the next mountain. What am I searching for? What defining moment started me on this quest? Was it a longing inside, a flash of some kind, maybe just curiosity? Whatever it was, it was compelling. There was never a choice, as if I was destined to do this.

Meditation

Begin with your three circling breaths. Then, instead of focusing on your solar plexus, focus on your nose tip by noticing that one, small area inside your nose near the tip or the rim where you feel the distinct sensation of your incoming breath. For the remainder of today's sessions, focus on the nose tip and let the body breathe naturally, except for an extended out breath. Don't force the in breath—wait for the body to breathe naturally. Remain concentrated on the feeling of your breath at the nose tip, which is now your concentration object replacing the solar plexus. Be aware at all times how the breath fills and floods the body, but remain anchored at the nose tip. If, however, you have a strong, reoccuring feeling to return to the solar plexus, do so. Follow your intuition, but be careful, the mind is tricky.

Personal Journal

_____
_____
_____
_____ *Date* _____

DAY 37

Insight

Blinded by sweetness and ease, he quickly became lost.

Reflections

Where have I learned my greatest lessons in life, when times were good or when I was blind-sided by disaster? I don't recall much of my childhood birthday parties, but I vividly remember watching in horror as my puppy was run over by a car when I was a child. The memory is indelibly etched in my mind...and I grew up a little that day.

Meditation

Continue your meditation exercises from the last session, always being compassionate with yourself. You've probably noticed that it is easier to locate the area where the breath touches inside your nose while breathing in rather than breathing out. If you lose track of the feeling and the area that it touches when exhaling, remember the feeling and where the area was, and stay there until you locate them again by inhaling. Keep in mind that the exhalation is longer than the inhalation, but other than that, the breathing should be natural. Always remain anchored at the nose tip but feel the breath cleansing your body as well.

Personal Journal

_____

_____

_____

_____ Date _____

DAY 38

Insight

Our relationship with ourselves, with nature, with others. What a brilliant mirror!

Reflections

Maybe on some magnificent day when I truly understand the way things are, I won't harbor the slightest thought of jealousy or hatred toward anybody. They say that thoughts precede words, words precede actions, and actions determine our fate in the next world. I can already see that at any given moment, there is either love or fear in my heart; there is not enough room for both. Which one is in my heart right now? I will reflect on this every moment, and perhaps this simple awareness, alone, will create changes in me.

Meditation

For today's sessions, don't do any concentration exercises, but instead, imagine yourself in a rain forest perched high in a tree. Underneath is a path that tigers use. Then picture each of your thoughts as a tiger walking beneath the tree. Be very careful not to jump onto the backs of any of these tigers and find yourself being carried away and eaten by them. Just watch the tigers come down the trail, pass below, and disappear over the hill. If no thoughts appear, carefully watch the path. Who or what is watching?

Personal Journal

_____
_____
_____
_____ Date _____

DAY 39

Insight

Jump in over your head!

Reflections

When will I throw caution to the wind and take a chance? It's as if I'm standing on a high cliff with untried wings, frightened, yet knowing that I'll never fly unless I jump.

Meditation

Now go back to your nose and concentrate carefully on the *feeling* of your breath in your nostrils, breathing as instructed. Do not *anticipate* the breath touching the inside of the nostrils; *experience* the touch and feeling each time as if for the first time. Everything must be experienced in the "now." This method of attention is termed "nose tip concentration." Feel the breath, not only at the nose tip, but throughout your entire body as if every inch of skin was breathing, not only the lungs. But your primary focus will remain at the nose tip, keeping thoughts at arm's length. If a thought does take control, causing you to lose your concentration, gently bring yourself back to your breath as soon as you discover that you've been abducted. It's common for thoughts to override your concentration in the beginning.

Personal Journal

_____

_____

_____

_____ *Date* _____

DAY 40

Insight

With eyes wide open, travel in intellectual and spiritual darkness.

Reflections

How can my background, my heritage, or my learning help me to become enlightened? Surely, there is no relationship. Relying on these things to help me now would be like studying algebra in preparation for my wedding night.

Meditation

Continue with nose tip concentration. Review each point carefully. The in breath is to be drawn into this area, then the out breath is two or three times longer. Maintain your concentration on the feeling and the exact area inside of the nose both while inhaling and exhaling, with each complete breath noticed in its entirety, but only in the background.

Personal Journal

_____
_____
_____
_____ _Date_ _____

DAY 41

Insight

One spark and the spiritual life catches fire.

Reflections

The misery in my life that I resist—does it hold me back or push me forward? I must carefully think this through. Does the moth resist opening its secure cocoon, unaware of wings that spread and the freedom of flight? Surely, we are all destined for freedom, regardless of our struggles. Isn't this what every creature aspires to?

Meditation

As the length of your sessions increase, you might want to alternate sitting and walking meditation. When practicing walking meditation, find a quiet, secluded place to walk. Except when practicing with a group, it is best to keep your practice to yourself and not make any exhibition, both during sitting and walking meditation. Walk back and forth in a natural manner at a slightly less-than-normal pace, with your hands clasped below your navel and your arms hanging heavy and relaxed from your shoulders. Keep your eyes down, not glancing around, and focused two paces ahead. A path 20 to 30 paces in length is good, laid out generally east to west or in the same direction the sun travels that season. (Sleeping head to foot in this direction is helpful as well.) Any distance, however, that can be accommodated either indoors or outdoors is fine. During your walking, you may stop at any time and stand still if you are so inclined, to strengthen your concentration or investigations. Continue nose tip concentration while walking for now. You will see yourself walking, but seemingly looking through your nose tip. Compare your concentration efforts during walking meditation with those of your sitting meditation.

Personal Journal

_____

_____

_____

_____ *Date* _____

DAY 42

Insight

Life is for living. Live to understand beyond a small mind.

Reflections

If I truly believe my present efforts will make a difference in the next world, where do my priorities lie? How much attention should I devote to my family's material support and how much to their emotional and spiritual development? Can I do both or does one steal from the other? I am so wrapped up in this idea of doing everything right. It is such a big responsibility. Am I beginning to realize that this whole idea of doing, and its never-ending conflicts, must be directly connected to the ultimate freedom I so desperately seek? It doesn't seem to be the doing that's troublesome, but rather the one doing it!

Meditation

Resume sitting practice now, beginning with your warm-up exercise and then your nose tip concentration. Remain vigilant, but relaxed...relaxed...relaxed.

Personal Journal

_____

_____

_____

_____ Date _____

DAY 43

Insight

I finished the puzzle, then threw it away.

Reflections

Once something no longer mystifies me, I'm through with it. The interest wanes and I can't wait to move on. I'm noticing lately that many things of this world that mystified me in the past are losing their glamour.

Meditation

Nose tip concentration involves noticing the incoming breath as it touches the inside of your nostrils. Concentrate intensely on the exact area where you feel this contact. The feeling and awareness of the breath are the important things. When you exhale, keep your attention focused on this sensation even though its sensitivity will diminish without the rush of the inhalation's incoming air. Keep your undivided attention here. Be vigilant; don't follow your breath in and out (but be aware of it) or allow extraneous thoughts to interfere with your focus. Stay on the area.

Personal Journal

_____

_____

_____

_____ Date _____

DAY 44

Insight

Wait.

Reflections

What is risked when I simply wait? Is non-action the most courageous of actions? Fear plays such a dominant role in my frenzied activities. At work, I rush around, afraid to be inefficient and not get things done in time; or I dash home, afraid of losing precious personal time. If my many fears could magically be dispelled, would I ever hurry again?

Meditation

When inhaling, always locate the area inside your nostrils where you feel your breath. Knowing that you are in this process of concentration, even while doing it, is an overview, a hint of momentary insight. If thoughts interfere and carry you away from your object of concentration, gently return to the area as soon as you realize that you have strayed. Remembering to return to the area and becoming acquainted with the many thoughts that interfere with your concentration and their patterns is mindfulness.

Personal Journal

_____
_____
_____
_____ Date _____

DAY 45

Insight

The wave was happy on the beach, but it couldn't stay.

Reflections

If I genuinely seek freedom, mustn't I eventually discover what imprisons me? If I painfully find that my jailers are the very people and things that I treasure, what should I do then? If I really desire liberation, must I change my feelings toward these cherished things? How could I continue to carry out my responsibilities toward them? Perhaps I needn't worry about this, however. Maybe, just maybe, at some point in my practice a new insight will arise. Would I then see that my treasuring of these things is no more than a selfish clinging, but has the potential to evolve into something much greater; an expansive love—a love so unconditional that it is completely self-sufficient, not dependent on any love in return? A love, similar to sunlight, that bathes everything, in which the people and things that I love are no longer jailers, but divine delights.

Meditation

Continue with your nose tip concentration. Always remember to begin your sessions with three circling breaths.

Personal Journal

_____

_____

_____

_____ Date _____

DAY 46

Insight

Everyday life: A curse? A blessing? A rock polisher grinding hard edges into polished gems?

Reflections

Ordinary life can be so dreary. I try to make it exciting but I seem to be swimming in molasses, just going through the motions. How could such an existence be the exact place that I need to be to find my freedom? My fledgling attempts to escape this dull existence never pan out for long, usually only compounding my problems and strengthening my resolve to find another way.

Meditation

Lengthen your sessions to 45 minutes now. Extend them longer if you prefer, but sit at least 45 minutes twice a day. Continue with your nose tip concentration.

Personal Journal

_____

_____

_____

_____ Date _____

DAY 47

Insight

The creative energy of emptiness, the imprisonment of belief.

Reflections

I'm only pretending to meditate, you know. I go through the motions of sitting still, but I really crave excitement. I can't wait to do things, because if I don't keep myself busy with one activity after another, that empty feeling creeps in. Then I become bored and despondent. I'm extremely clever at escaping boredom. I'm so good at it that I've never really had to explore my emptiness. Deep inside, I know that facing this emptiness reveals an unknown depth. But the fact is, truth, this unknown depth, is still far too frightening for my non-insightful mind to face. I can't help wondering, however, what it would be like to have a mind that was empty of all the excess baggage, but incredibly aware.

Meditation

Continue with your nose tip concentration. It is important to recognize the thinking process as a process, not as you, and that you begin to understand it. Remember, try not to think about, analyze, or categorize a thought once you become aware of it—simply drop it. The more important a thought seems to be, the more crucial it is to let it go. Just return to your calm breath.

Personal Journal

_____

_____

_____

_____ Date _____

DAY 48

Insight

Waves brushing the shore, returning to their Source.

Reflections

I was at the beach today. As I was watching the waves lazily roll in, I noticed that although no individual wave touches the beach twice, the sea is always there creating more waves. Are the waves jealous of each other, or are they in harmony? The ocean doesn't seem to mind how they feel; it carries them all.

Meditation

If your mind is very active, so active in fact that you find it impossible to remain concentrated on the area in your nose, you might consider using a counting technique, temporarily, to help still the commotion. To do this, count backward after each exhalation; for example, first inhale, and then on the exhalation, count "ten." Inhale, exhale, count "nine," and so forth. When you inhale, concentrate on the breath in your nose; when you exhale, picture the number in your mind. Not losing track of the number order verifies that you are concentrating. After your practice becomes established, you might want to occasionally begin at 100 and count backward to test yourself, confirming that you can keep your thoughts at bay. For this practice period, try the backward counting technique starting at 20 and see what progress you've made in dismissing thoughts (if you lose count, start over from the beginning). When you have successfully finished the counting, continue with nose tip concentration. Don't forget, your out breath is always longer than the in breath.

Personal Journal

_____

_____

_____

_____ Date _____

DAY 49

Insight

Silence is the bridge.

Reflections

When I'm with my friends and the conversation lulls, the silence is awkward. It is as if, unless we constantly entertain each other, we fail in some strange way. Entertainment has taken over my life, actually, and any kind of austerity is the farthest thing from my mind, but what is austerity, exactly? Living in a cave? Maybe austerity is more refined than that. Maybe there is much more at stake than I realize.

Meditation

Continue with nose tip concentration. Begin today's sessions by using the backward-counting technique, starting from 30.

Personal Journal

_____

_____

_____

_____ Date _____

DAY 50

Insight

Quiet minds walk among the clamor undisturbed.

Reflections

Now I see! The trick is to remain in the muck while rising above it, like water lilies growing in a muddy pond. Is this possible for me? It is easy to remain serene in peaceful surroundings, but difficult when immersed in bedlam. Perhaps someday when I find that ellusive peace that I know is hidden deep inside, outward circumstances won't matter.

Meditation

Continue your nose tip concentration. Only count until excessive thinking subsides.

Personal Journal

_____

_____

_____

_____ Date _____

DAY 51

Insight

Truth is precious. Many risk their lives for it, let alone their fortunes.

Reflections

Everything around me is changing. It is as if I don't fit in anymore, that I had somehow moved on while everything else hadn't. I am a fish out of water that longs to swim home, but no longer knows where home is. My wonderful life surrounds me, so why do I feel so alienated and alone? Nobody understands. I can't even express what I'm feeling because I don't understand it myself.

Meditation

Let's review your posture: Sit upright with the small of your back curved naturally in, hips thrust forward. You may keep your eyes closed, or half closed gazing at the floor 3 or 4 feet ahead. Your neck should be stretched upwards, with the chin tucked in slightly. Your face, shoulders, and stomach should be relaxed, with your left hand under the right, either thumbs touching lightly or circles formed with your thumbs and index fingers. Be certain your head is not tilting forward or backward, or that your clothes are not too tight or warm. Now continue with nose tip concentration.

Personal Journal

_____

_____

_____

_____ Date _____

DAY 52

Insight

The mind seeks freedom; release it from its bonds of attachment.

Reflections

Why am I so hesitant to follow my heart? What's the worst that could happen? If today, I could do exactly as I pleased with no consequences, what would I do? The problem is, I don't know how to do something that wouldn't cause me problems, because I would surely be following my head instead of my heart. How will I ever be able to change? How can I learn to listen to my heart?

Meditation

Continue with nose tip concentration. Use the counting technique only if thoughts are a constant nuisance.

Personal Journal

_____

_____

_____

_____ Date _____

DAY 53

Insight

Whatever arises will pass. What is eternal will always be.

Reflections

Is there a part of me that is eternal? Can I know that part? I'm beginning to feel that I am no longer alone, that something is there. I can't prove this, but somehow I just know it, without a doubt. Many possibilities must exist beyond my mind, and to discover them, I know that I must let go of the parts that are not eternal. Only then might another possibility enter my life.

Meditation

For some people, sudden things can occur during meditation practice, though not everybody experiences this. These things are usually not in any way an indication of progress. They are only interesting things that can come up and should be dropped immediately. Your body might begin shaking involuntarily, or you could see visions and hear voices. For example, you might see three shafts of light accompanied by a statement, "We are taking care of you." Unusual things such as these can present themselves without warning. For now, if anything happens out of the ordinary, don't become enthralled or horrified—and don't try to repeat it! This only slows progress. Continue as if nothing has happened, no matter how wonderful or frightening these things are. Keep yourself grounded in the reality of the touch of your breath. Carry on with nose tip concentration.

Personal Journal

_____

_____

_____

_____ Date _____

DAY 54

Insight

A mere glimpse will spoil everything.

Reflections

If I become caught in indecision, with one foot in this world and one in the next, I'll be miserable! Before I climb up on the stage and peek behind the curtains, I'd better be prepared to walk away from the audience.

Meditation

As your practice develops, the simple effort of applying your mind to a concentration object, which in this case is the feeling of the breath in your nose, will draw you into deeper stages of meditation.

Personal Journal

_____

_____

_____

_____ _Date_ _____

DAY 55

Insight

The unknown—to be approached eagerly, not fearfully.

Reflections

I'm about to embark upon intense meditation that I've heard can be dangerous to a coarse mind. I really don't know who I am yet. Do I have limited ambitions, few wants, and a kind heart? However, when I think about it, I'm probably safe. Would a cruel, insensitive heart still be involved with this guide?

Meditation

Certain experiences oftentimes bridge the physical and spiritual world. One of these will be discussed shortly—one that you may have already experienced. It results from repeatedly applying your mind to a concentration object. During today's practice, continue with your nose tip concentration.

Personal Journal

_____

_____

_____

_____ Date _____

DAY 56

Insight

She fought for power and wealth, but entered the next world impoverished—with no power, no wealth, and with no understanding.

Reflections

A heart of gold. What an interesting expression because gold is so cold and heavy. How can I warm and lighten my heart? Better yet, do I have the courage to empty it of my illusions?

Meditation

Continue your regular practice—three deep, circular breaths followed by nose tip concentration. At times, it can be a struggle to keep your attention on the feeling of the breath every moment as your mind drifts here and there.

Personal Journal

_____

_____

_____

_____ Date _____

A Year to Enlightenment

DAY 57

Insight

Direct experience! Dust now gathers on my many books.

Reflections

Will I ever come face to face with that...something? That which never began and will never end? Is it inside me, waiting patiently to be discovered? How innocent and vulnerable must I become to sneak beneath the heavy veil of myself and glimpse its brilliance?

Meditation

After you become proficient and confident in directing your attention to the feeling of your breath, questions and doubts melt away. With this assurance, meditation deepens. Concerns about protecting yourself dissolve, letting you relax into the practice instead of fighting it. Tie your mind firmly to the feeling of your breath as it touches the inside of your nose and permeates your body. Remain steadfast as you continue your nose tip concentration.

Personal Journal

_____

_____

_____

_____ *Date* _____

DAY 58

Insight

Observations remembered become knowledge. Knowledge becomes falsehoods.

Reflections

What do I usually think about? My plans, my hopes for a better life perhaps? At times, I think about my problems, or how I can improve myself. Actually, when I think about it, I think constantly, and what I think about is usually myself. What is it about me that's so compelling—my intelligence, my energy, my good fortune? These things ensure my success in the world, but what happens when that intelligence and energy begin to wane, or bad luck strikes? What then? And what exactly is this me or myself that I'm so obsessed with? What if me vanished? I am trusting that my guide will explore these things with me.

Meditation

Work diligently on your nose tip concentration. Your mind will stop fighting itself at some point and absorb into the moment. This is a state of not knowing. Whenever you think that you know something, the "thinking that you know" is merely a reflection of the self, which is storing dead information in your files. Your knowledge, therefore, is no longer alive; it is merely stale memories. It happened. It's history. It isn't happening. Understand that the something you are seeking can never be found in the past, which is dead. The past is where memories and knowledge are buried. That something can only be found in this immense, vibrant, and alive moment where time no longer exists, where creativity originates, and where the self can never be found.

Personal Journal

_____
_____
_____
_____ Date _____

A Year to Enlightenment

DAY 59

Insight

Dreams can seem so real; this life of ours.

Reflections

Sometimes I feel that I'm blindly stumbling from one thing to another, leaving no lasting impact. Everything is steadily receding into my past. What is the true significance of my life?

Meditation

As a beginner, you might feel dissatisfied and dull at times. Doubts will come up. This is the mind's self-defense mechanism attempting to discourage you from meditating. Doubt, at times, appears in the form of metaphysical questions that the mind cannot possibly know: Is the universe eternal or not eternal? Is there a soul or not? Do I continue after death? These questions will drive you mad because you will find numerous, conflicting answers in books, only confusing you more. This will continue until you realize that the one who is questioning is and has been the problem, and that meditation offers a permanent cure for this. A time will come when these questions lose their importance. They will be dwarfed by something greater that will leave no room for doubt whatsoever. During these initial times of doubt, however, you will only notice the long, dry periods during which nothing seems to be happening. You will not be aware that the fog of confusion is subtly lifting. These dry periods are to be expected. Know that the mere attempt to meditate, even without apparent results, has a profound influence on your spiritual life regardless of whether you are aware of its influences or not. How you feel about your progress rarely is an indication of your development. Your effort is what counts, so try not to evaluate your work. Stay true to your nose tip concentration.

Personal Journal

_____

_____

_____

_____ Date _____

DAY 60

Insight

Why all this? Why not just nothing?

Reflections

I do have questions: What is the purpose of life? Is it conflict? Why do I exist; is it only to suffer? Surely there must be some other reason that I'm alive, some kind of connection...to something. Can I ever let go of these questions? Can I actually trust that someday the answers won't be important? Perhaps my guide is right, maybe someday the answers won't be necessary. Who or what is it that questions?

Meditation

The results of meditation can be subtle, perhaps a minor insight connected with your daily routine where you might suddenly see a more efficient way to perform a task, or notice something from a different perspective such as an awareness of your emotions. At other times, meditation can be remarkable and rather spectacular, when your life might take a dramatic turn, or you might see visions, brilliant flashes of white light, colors, or loud, prophetic teachings. The important thing is to watch every meditation experience come and go without being caught up in it. In the end, unusual meditation experiences are no different from taking the scenic route—your journey might take a little longer but will be more interesting, regardless of whether your experiences are non-existent, subtle, or dramatic. However, you will definitely arrive at your destination. Continue with your nose tip concentration.

Personal Journal

_____

_____

_____

_____ Date _____

DAY 61

Insight

Teaching what we know is deceit. Teaching what we are is truth.

Reflections

Meditation is certainly unique. Although far removed from any particular religion or belief, it accommodates them all. It helps me get beyond my petty self toward my essence, that eternal something with no beginning. We have many names for this, but I prefer an ecumenical word, such as "essence" or "Source." There may be disagreements about its name or description, but how can words begin to describe something so profound, something that can only be truly understood in our hearts?

Meditation

Meditation might bring up fearful thoughts connected to illness and death, and the sooner these types of feelings are put to rest, the better. You have successfully skirted around this fear in the past by ignoring it and not looking at it directly, but now you must face it straight away! Visions, voices, lights, or anything else you might see or hear should be courteously, gently, but firmly dismissed as well. Just return to your breath. The root of this fear is a misunderstanding about yourself—you might not be who or what you think you are. During today's sessions, use the backward counting technique after each exhalation to check your progress with concentration. Count from 100 back to one. If you lose count, begin again until you complete the sequence. Then go back to your regular nose tip concentration.

Personal Journal

_____

_____

_____

_____ Date _____

DAY 62

Insight

Spirit is chaos to a structured mind.

Reflections

Spiritual seeds sprout from tiny cracks in the hard pavement of my controlled life. It is those little interruptions—the accident, the illness, perhaps a death—that opens doors for me. Why can't I step through?

Meditation

Your mind loves to entertain itself endlessly with memories and daydreams. It is not at all interested in being in this moment by practicing meditation. Because your mind perceives the moment as empty, it is intimidated by it, so you will find yourself involved in an ongoing struggle to restrain your mind's wanderings and bring it back to your concentration. As you continue with your nose tip concentration, remember three things: one, that the feeling of your breath in the area where your breath touches the inside of your nose is your concentration object; two, to always be completely in the moment and see and feel everything as if for the first time; three, to watch the area in your nose as you would watch a knife in the hand of an assailant—with the utmost attention.

Personal Journal

_____
_____
_____
_____ Date _____

DAY 63

Insight

Concentration. Mindfulness. Insight....Inseparable.

Reflections

Awe-inspiring beauty, close encounters with death, heart-breaking disappointments, life-threatening tragedies, spiritual awakenings; these kinds of things overwhelm my everyday mind and reduce me to tears as their truths touch me directly. They are glimpses of reality that bypass my mind and directly affect my heart, creating permanent shifts in the depths of my being, changing my values forever, and launching my life into uncharted waters. But how do I then deepen these experiences in order to approach enlightenment?

Meditation

Practice nose tip concentration. Review your posture and make sure that you remain relaxed. Don't overlook your preliminary circling breaths.

Personal Journal

_____
_____•_____
_____
_____ _Date_ _____

DAY 64

Insight

Sleep; deeper than the dream world of our lives.

Reflections

I'm so relieved when I wake up from a bad dream. Is life a dream as well? How many layers of dreams are there? At times, I wish I could wake up and discover that my life was just a bad dream; perhaps this is what the next world promises. At other times, I love my life and never want it to end, but end it must—and then what?

Meditation

You are now ready to refine your nose tip concentration. Imagine waves washing over a rock lying on a sandy beach. Similar to waves washing over the rock, imagine each breath washing over your focus area inside the nose. Your inhalation is an incoming wave, and your long exhalation, a receding wave. Your attention is constantly on the feeling of your breath and the rock, or the area inside your nose, never following the waves or the breath. But you must, out of the corner of your eye, distinguish between an incoming wave and a receding wave, and know whether you are inhaling or exhaling. Be particularly aware of the exhale, which is longer than the inhale, and notice the pause after the exhalation before the inhalation begins, all the while keeping the feeling of your breath as the primary focus, as well as the area where it touches.

Personal Journal

_____
_____
_____
_____ Date _____

DAY 65

Insight

Love only happens beyond our control.

Reflections

I have made an interesting discovery: My knowledge and learning are mere imagery, and this imagery has replaced reality in my mind. This is what is holding me back in this spiritual business; the imagery that replaced reality. For my long journey ahead, I promise to follow my intuitive heart instead of my head, letting everything else fall by the wayside. If I can keep this promise, and if I can separate deception from actuality, I'll find my freedom.

Meditation

You now have three things to concentrate on: one, the feeling of the breath touching the inside of your nose (the crucial thing is the feeling); two, keeping track of whether it is an in breath or an out breath as it washes past the area and permeates your body, flooding it with calm energy; three, concentrating on the area where your breath touches the inside of your nose, never following the breath around or in and out, but still knowing whether it is an in breath or an out breath. Make certain that the out breath is longer than the in breath, and notice the momentary pause between the inhale and exhale.

Personal Journal

_____

_____

_____

_____ *Date* _____

DAY 66

Insight

Intuitive hearts know. Emotional hearts sow.

Reflections

Intuitive persuasions are nudging me in directions that aren't necessarily making sense to my logical mind. These urges appear as small, silent voices in my heart, quiet and unassuming in one way, but surprisingly powerful in another. These tiny voices are extremely delicate and easily overwhelmed by the dominant voice of logic, so I must be discerning when choosing which voice to follow. Everything that's creative, insightful, and spontaneous seems to come from these small, silent voices. Logic, on the other hand, speaks to me about function and technicalities.

Meditation

During meditation, it is vital to be completely immersed in the moment, a moment in which you will see everything as if for the first time. But the moment is fast, and you won't have time to think about it. Every intuitive experience during practice will eventually be integrated into your life, simply because meditation, as you will soon discover, is always a direct expression of your life. When outdoors, especially in nature, keep your mind absent of verbalizations (thoughts that appear as if you are chatting to yourself). An excellent practice is to be aware of your breathing at all times, no matter what you are doing. You will learn to distinguish when thought is appropriate and when thought merely muddies up your insight. You are now beginning to alter entrenched, destructive habits. Soon, your anger and many obsessive desires will lessen noticeably, and when they are gone, what will you be left with? Continue with your nose tip concentration.

Personal Journal

_____

_____

_____

_____ Date _____

DAY 67

Insight

Suffering exists in the world.

Reflections

When I long for something and can't get it, I become frustrated. When I finally do acquire it, then I soon become annoyed because I'm afraid I'll lose it. Eventually, I find myself doing extraordinarily heroic things to hold on to my property and protect it. In some ways, I become imprisoned by it because I so desperately need it for my happiness. Later, of course, I grow weary of it and perhaps want it out of my life, but what if I then can't get rid of it? Now the irritation increases.

Meditation

Until insight arises, danger always exists in the appearance of psychological attachment to the form of this practice, but you can never become attached to the truth it reveals. Truth moves far too fast for you to hold it. When there is nothing but the feeling of your breath in your nose, that moment is real; that moment is truth. Forsake the limitations of the past and the uncertainty of the future; simply remain in this moment—right here, right now. Continue with your nose tip concentration.

Personal Journal

_____

_____

_____

_____ Date _____

DAY 68

Insight

The cause of our tremendous, never-ending suffering? It is simply wanting.

Reflections

Whenever I achieve something, I feel great, I feel exuberant, but the accomplishment is short-lived, fleeting, and momentary; just a brief respite from my incessant wanting. In no time, I go after something else. Why couldn't I feel exuberant always, without first having to achieve something? What's stopping me from living freely every moment?

Meditation

Be cautious of spiritual ambition. Sit quietly with no agenda, accompanied only by your five true companions—humility, self-sacrifice, compassion, generosity, and restraint. Continue with your nose tip concentration.

Personal Journal

_____
_____
_____
_____ Date _____

DAY 69

Insight

The steps to end our suffering are simple...beginning with an acknowledgment that we suffer.

Reflections

How can I end my endless conflicts? The choices that I'm forced to make every day can be daunting, and filled with conflict. Why can't I live a choiceless life? It is so frustrating. Maybe this is how life is, but I would prefer less turmoil. But perhaps there is no escape. Maybe I have yet to learn my first great lesson—that humankind suffers terribly in so many ways. If only I could learn not to place so much importance on the results of my choices. Why must I always win and not lose? My desires seem as endless as the choices I must make.

Meditation

Continue practicing diligently, expecting nothing in return. Don't strive. Sit quietly and peacefully. The thoughts that appear are not your enemies, for thinking is just one of many duties your mind performs in order to keep your body functioning and protected. Look at thoughts now as belonging to somebody else, as you gradually break your personal association with them. Remember that your body is temporary, as is your mind, so never become overly attached to either. Continue with your nose tip concentration.

Personal Journal

_____

_____

_____

_____ *Date* _____

DAY 70

Insight

There is a unique suffering, the only kind that will end suffering.

Reflections

Maybe when I really take time to first admit, and then understand my aggravations, I can end them. I must seriously get into this by talking about it, applying my mind to it, and somehow discovering virtue within myself. I can already see that this will require not only living sanely, but also pushing myself to see even deeper, really thinking beyond what is apparent, and, of course, meditating.

Meditation

Repeatedly return to the feeling of the breath in your nose and throughout your body. See your incoming breath and your outgoing breath as waves washing over a rock on the beach. Know every movement of your breath but remain fixed on that rock where the feeling arises. It is incorrect to think that this practice will lead to further attainments. You must practice as if you are going to be aware of the feeling of your breath for eternity, expecting nothing in return. This exercise will produce astonishing results over time, but not if anticipated. If you wait for results, you lose the essence of your practice, which is to be in the moment.

Personal Journal

_____

_____

_____

_____ *Date* _____

DAY 71

Insight

A vacancy within the fabric of space, or within the fabric of our lives, is soon filled again.

Reflections

The planet I call home is such a tiny dot, revolving around our sun, and the sun itself is merely one of billions of suns clustered in a galaxy. Then there are uncountable galaxies populating the universe—and beyond this universe, perhaps billions more. Who knows what unimaginable things exist? The immensity of time and space is overwhelming, beyond comprehension. Astrophysicists say the universe began with something very small, about the size of a pea, almost nothing. Sages agree, saying that from nothing arises everything and within everything is nothing. The more I learn about my world, the more science and spirituality blur, but the real question is not about the universe, it is about me. Can I ever remain empty without attempting to fill the void? Perhaps I can, but only when I move beyond my mind.

Meditation

Thoughts can be distracting during practice. They bring up fear as well as questioning and doubt—things you live with every day. Your mind is simply not capable of highest understanding—but something else is; trust your meditation, it will take you there. Continue with your nose tip concentration. Don't forget your preliminary exercises.

Personal Journal

_____

_____

_____

_____ Date _____

DAY 72

Insight

Never hurry, never worry.

Reflections

How can I simplify my life a tad more? Can I find a few more moments for stillness within my manic activities? My life rushes from one thing to another, and any attempt to slow it down seems unworkable at times. My life is like an ever-present lust with endless desires to be fulfilled. My mind actually doesn't want to slow down. It must stay ahead of the increasingly steep wave it is creating for fear of becoming awash in its wake. Why do I push so much? If I could only relax and do each thing well and completely, wouldn't life present me with what really needs to be done, without so many excesses?

Meditation

If a mind remains distracted and worried, perhaps caught up in sensual lust or resentment and agitation, lost in doubt which causes endless questioning, then your effort to meditate will be like entering a filthy bathroom—your spiritual tendencies will immediately turn around and walk out! Look at your life. Make adjustments. Induced discipline might be the only solution for the time being to keep you out of trouble until a natural discipline develops. Continue with your nose tip concentration.

Personal Journal

_____
_____
_____
_____ *Date* _____

DAY 73

Insight

Pity the seeker, but pity more those who love their life, for soon it will change.

Reflections

How can I explain this yearning in my heart, this feeling that I'm on my way home but have forgotten where home is, or how to get there? Is it possible that a psychic, unconscious memory of my spiritual roots is drawing me back? Is it by negation that I discover the little tricks in life that constantly fool me and make me forget—little tricks, like the falsehood of permanence, the promised happiness that always slips through my fingers like water, and the myth of something substantial behind it all? Are these things pushing me to search for truth?

Meditation

Whatever occurs in meditation, let it be. By reviewing or trying to repeat experiences, or perhaps feeling proud or self-righteous about them, you will impede progress. Experiences become history the moment they happen, and the past can never survive in the immediacy of this precious moment. Similar to a person who goes to work every day to the same job and returns home to the same routine with no excitement whatsoever in his or her life, you, as a meditator, will patiently persevere as well. Just think of the horrible things people do to get out of work or create constant excitement in their lives—stealing, lying, and even killing each other. As a meditator and a warrior, it is your duty to face your responsibilities and reject inclinations to escape. It is just you and the feeling of your breath, hour after hour, day after day. You disappear; there is only the breath, arising and passing. Continue with your nose tip concentration.

Personal Journal

_____

_____

_____

_____ Date _____

DAY 74

Insight

To find, stop seeking!

Reflections

Can I live my life by watching everything clearly, through the fog of my thoughts, my stale memories, my judgments? Without old images and the excess baggage I carry on my back? Can I throw the entire lot out for a brief insightful second and truly look with eyes wide open, see life as it is, see the truth of it, see the beauty of it, see the disgust of it, but never push it away nor hold it dear? If only I could experience everything...but grasp nothing.

Meditation

Cultivate a mind that can focus, undisturbed, on the feeling of the breath inside your nostrils and throughout your body. Strike the bell (bring your attention to the feeling of the breath as often as possible), night or day. Keep striking the bell until it becomes a single, uninterrupted tone no longer requiring constant striking. When you can do this, it will feel as if you are falling into your meditation object, where you will be able to remain without disturbance.

Personal Journal

_____

_____

_____

_____ Date _____

DAY 75

Insight

In this world, we are required to carry rocks on our backs, but not in our hearts.

Reflections

As a human being, have I advanced beyond incalculable odds to an incredible state where I have acquired the intelligence and potential to hunger for my roots—that spiritual essence from which I have sprung? I think that I have. At one time, I mistakenly believed the promises of humankind, not grasping the immensity of the Source of all things, thinking that the world itself could satisfy my longing. All of my energy was spent toying with things of the world, suffering untold disappointments as I struggled to acquire this and that, hoping for fulfillment and happiness, but finding myself looking in all the wrong places.

Meditation

You have been taking three deep, circling breaths. On the next page, a second opening procedure, a seven-step exercise which balances your practice and your life, will be explained. Both the three deep breaths and your new, seven-step exercise will only take a minute or two each day, and will be your standard warm-up before beginning most sessions. Please follow the instructions carefully. For today, however, continue with your nose tip concentration.

Personal Journal

_____

_____

_____

_____ Date _____

DAY 76

Insight

An ocean in each drop; the essence in each heart.

Reflections

I walked through fresh snow last night under brilliant stars that only appear on cold nights. How has such beauty escaped me? What have I been doing with my life? I can't even remember now. What really lies beyond all this, beyond my imagination?

Meditation

You will now start learning your new opening exercise. After your three circling breaths, begin with a slow inhalation, visualized as a ball of white light, moving from your tailbone, up your back, and ending a few inches above your head. As you exhale, imagine the white light showering sparks and bathing your body in its light. On the next inhalation, draw one-third of the inhalation into your forehead above and between your eyes, and at the same time let the ball of light descend into this forehead area, both lighting the area and opening it like petals of a flower. Draw the second one-third of the inhalation into your throat below your Adam's apple, and let the ball of light that is in your forehead descend down into the throat area, lighting and opening the area. Draw the final one-third of the inhalation into your heart, letting the ball of light descend into your heart. Hold the breath in your heart for 10 seconds, while visualizing the white ball of light expanding to first envelop your heart, then your body, and then the entire universe encompassing all things. Return to your nose tip concentration. When your sessions end today, close the three centers that you have opened in reverse order. Visualize closing each one, as a flower folds, beginning with your heart and ending with your forehead, but leave the top of the head open. It is important to close each of these centers after each session.

Personal Journal

_____

_____

_____

_____ Date _____

DAY 77

Insight

Only pure minds safely open themselves to that which is unknown.

Reflections

Hints of truth uncovered by meditation bypass my mind and directly influence my heart. These glimpses are creating permanent shifts in the depths of my being, changing my values and channeling my life into unexplored waters. Strong feelings are coming up now for no particular reason and are quite overwhelming at times, as if I am close to a breakthrough.

Meditation

Begin this session with your customary three deep, circling breaths, followed by the first three steps of the new exercise as mentioned previously. The fourth step begins with releasing the breath that you are holding at your heart, but release only one third of it. Drop this partial, one-third exhalation and the ball of light from your heart into your solar plexus (just above the navel. Now, open your solar plexus, similar to a flower, with an in breath and white light by inhaling completely the one-third out breath from the heart. For step five, exhale completely, dropping the breath and the white light from your solar plexus to the pubic area (this might be felt as a tingling in the sex organs). Now, flood that area with white light and breath, and open it, similar to a flower, by inhaling fully. This concludes the first five steps. You will learn the last two on the next day. Continue with nose tip concentration for the remainder of today's sessions. At the conclusion of practice, remember to close these areas, as a flower folds in the evening, beginning with the pubic area, then the solar plexus, heart, throat, and forehead—in that exact order. Leave the crown center open.

Personal Journal

_____

_____

_____

_____ Date _____

DAY 78

Insight

It resides at your base, waiting to be released.

Reflections

My mind must be as clean as a home ready for houseguests, and my heart must remain open, prepared to accept that which is my spiritual essence. I'm about to take serious steps that will radically affect my destiny, steps involving deep-seated changes and sweeping transformations.

Meditation

Now let's add the last two steps of your new, seven-step exercise. Reviewing step five, you filled and opened the pubic area with an inhalation and white light. For step six, exhale completely, dropping your breath and the white light to the base of your spine near the coccyx area. Fill this area and open it with a complete inhalation of white light, opening it like a flower. Then, as the area bathes in that light, exhale completely. Step seven brings your next inhalation and the light up your spine again, stopping at an area just above the top or crown of your head, where you will fill this area with volumes of white light and breath and open it. Then, as you exhale, reaffirm your intention to open yourself completely to your spiritual essence. This concludes your seven-step exercise. Practice these seven steps for about 10 minutes today before continuing with nose tip concentration. At the conclusion of practice, don't forget to always close these areas (fold the petals of the flowers), starting at the bottom of your spine, then the pubic area, solar plexus, heart, throat, and forehead. Always keep the crown of the head open and filled with light.

Personal Journal

_____

_____

_____

_____ *Date* _____

DAY 79

Insight

When you stop soaring, look closely at your broken wings.

Reflections

I'm determined to discover what's holding me back. What if I don't know what it is?

Meditation

Let's review your new exercise. Draw one-third of the inhalation into your forehead just above and between your eyes, and let the ball of light that is above your head descend into this forehead area. Draw the second one-third of the inhalation into your throat below your Adam's apple, and at the same time let the ball of light descend down into the throat area. Draw the final one-third of the inhalation into your heart, letting the ball of light descend there. Hold the breath in your heart for 10 seconds. The fourth step begins with releasing one-third of the breath that you are holding at your heart. Drop this one-third exhalation, and the ball of light, into your solar plexus. Fill your solar plexus with an in breath and white light by inhaling the one-third breath completely. For step five, exhale completely, dropping the breath and the white light from your solar plexus to the pubic area. Fill that area with white light and inhale fully. For step six, exhale completely, dropping your breath and the white light to the base of your spine near the coccyx area. Fill this area with a complete inhalation of white light and open it. Exhale completely. Step seven brings your inhalation and the light up your spine, stopping at an area just above the top of your head that you will fill with volumes of white light and open it. Practice these seven steps for about 10 minutes before continuing with nose tip concentration. At the conclusion of practice, close these areas, starting at the bottom of your spine, then the pubic area, solar plexus, heart, throat, and forehead. Always keep the crown of your head open and filled with light.

Personal Journal

_____

_____

_____

_____ *Date* _____

DAY 80

Insight

Travel light.

Reflections

An extended camping trip involves trudging many miles through rugged terrain while carrying all my supplies on my back. Wouldn't I carefully select what I bring along, leaving unnecessary things behind? What will I take with me to the other world? What will I leave behind?

Meditation

Begin your new seven-step opening today. It will feel clumsy at first, but soon will flow easily and quickly. This exercise, preceded by your three deep preliminary breaths, will begin most practice sessions. Don't forget: The areas must be closed, and in the correct order, after every session, with the exception of the crown which remains open and filled with light. Now continue with your nose tip concentration.

Personal Journal

_____

_____

_____

_____ Date _____

DAY 81

Insight

Artists paint images; sages paint reality.

Reflections

After a good night's sleep, won't I wake up with yesterday's passions and cravings extending into today? Would waking up in the next world be any different? It is not certain that I will magically be transformed into a saint! What if only my mind survives in the next world? What will I do with all of my physical cravings? I would be little more than a ravenous being, with a large stomach, and no mouth!

Meditation

Begin with your three circling breaths followed by your seven-step exercise, and then proceed with nose tip concentration. Focus on the touch of your breath, and on the exact area where it is felt in your nostrils. Each time you breathe in, establish the feeling of the new breath. Watch it as if for the first time, every time. Try to establish the feeling during your in breath and retain the feeling when you breathe out, then reestablish it on the next in breath. Don't create an image in your mind of the feeling, or of the area where it is felt, but rather focus on the actual feeling of your breath touching the area. Releasing images that form in meditation will help you release images you create in life. If the feeling seems to drift away from the inside of the nose, for example, if it moves into the forehead or into the heart, don't disturb your concentration by attempting to reposition it back into your nose. This only creates conflict. Stay focused on the feeling, and let it travel where it may. At the end of today's sessions, remember always to close each of the six centers in the correct order.

Personal Journal

_____

_____

_____

_____ *Date* _____

DAY 82

Insight

Can the simple answer be...sitting quietly?

Reflections

Let's see, what would be the advantages of not having senses such as seeing, smelling, hearing, tasting, and touching? For one thing, I wouldn't be concerned about making a living or accumulating money because I wouldn't need food or shelter. And I needn't worry about my health because physical pain, aging, and death, as I know it, would not exist. The only problems remaining would be mental, perhaps in the form of lingering desires, memories, plans, and projections, but isn't that what I'm working on in meditation?

Meditation

The seven areas that you are opening before practice each have different aspects. The area between your eyes stimulates spiritual vision, clairvoyance, and imparts a unique capacity to control difficult situations. After your preliminary exercises, imagine opening the forehead center and flooding it with light. Concentrate on this forehead center between your eyes for about a minute before resuming your regular nose tip practice. Always keep the in breath natural and the out breath extended when concentrating on any area.

Personal Journal

_____
_____
_____
_____ Date _____

DAY 83

Insight

One doesn't have to travel far to find a perfect hell.

Reflections

Two things continue to hold me hostage. If I had truly nothing to lose, fear and death would not intimidate me, but I have plans, right? My life is incomplete. When death does come, however, won't that very instant be real, alive, unknown? Isn't my concept of death, and my thoughts and opinions of death, the only things that are fearful? Fear can't possibly exist in this moment. It only has power when lurking in the shadows of my past, and in the nightmares of my future.

Meditation

Don't be surprised if concentration on your throat triggers flashes of random scenes and radiant waves of brilliant colors, so deep that you can barely stand it. The throat pathway also has the power to eliminate disease, inspire happiness, and refine thoughts. After your preliminary exercises today, imagine your throat opening and filling with light. Concentrate on your throat for about a minute before resuming nose tip concentration.

Personal Journal

_____

_____

_____

_____ Date _____

DAY 84

Insight

When you create a monster, you must feed it. If you don't, it will eat you.

Reflections

Without fully understanding my mind's desires, passions, thoughts, and my mind's concepts of me, won't I be utterly terrorized when I wake up someday without a body? If I could truly comprehend these things, wouldn't I lose my fear of death? When I think about it, my body already disappears when I sit motionless during meditation. This practice is mysterious indeed. To what could it be leading?

Meditation

The heart center initially is the center of your bright awareness. It instills courage, regulates the immune system, and brings up deep feelings of compassion as well as promoting an understanding of your own mind. Here, you will see quite clearly that no matter where this practice leads, you will be protected. Your minimal physical requirements will be met, provided your practice is energetic and sincere. A word of caution: When working with these seven centers, the acquisition of supernormal powers is possible, which would stymie an immature practice. So if your goal is to attain full enlightenment, be careful you don't create things that are difficult to dismantle. After finishing your preliminary exercises, concentrate on your heart for about a minute, opening it and filling with it with light, before resuming your nose tip concentration.

Personal Journal

_____

_____

_____

_____ Date _____

A Year to Enlightenment

DAY 85

Insight

The difference between youth and old age? The breadth of a gray hair.

Reflections

I see with these eyes, but when my eyes are gone, what will I see with? Perhaps I will only see memories. Is there a seeing beyond my past and future?

Meditation

Your solar plexus can bring up very strange visions of indescribable places, and dreams of flying effortlessly, leaving you breathless, and wondering why you never attempted to fly before. It seems so easy! Focusing on your solar plexus can also reduce physical and mental pain, and mystically acquaint you with physical aspects of the body without the bother of studying anatomy. If, however, you happen to find yourself traveling around in space, return to your concentration and disregard this form of entertainment. It will not help toward your goal of understanding. When you are finished with your preliminary exercises, imagine your solar plexus opening and filling with light. Concentrate on your solar plexus for about a minute before resuming your nose tip concentration.

Personal Journal

_____

_____

_____

_____ Date _____

DAY 86

Insight

See it clearly, but never look for it.

Reflections

I study my mind during meditation and I magically change. Who would believe that such an indirect action really works? Some things haven't changed yet, but I'm becoming aware of what they are now. This, in itself, moves me in new directions.

Meditation

After finishing your preliminary exercises, imagine your pubic area opening and filling with light. Concentrate on the pubic area for a minute or so before starting nose tip concentration. This region is connected to uncontrolled worldly desires, but odd, intuitive urges can crop up from here as well, both threatening and liberating, and you could become caught in the middle.

Personal Journal

_____

_____

_____

_____ *Date* _____

DAY 87

Insight

Write all your wisdom down, in the sand at low tide.

Reflections

Could I live in a cave for three years and come out refreshed, ready to return for another three? Or if stranded on a desert island, what couldn't I do without? Providing I had the bare necessities, could I merely sit down and meditate? I'm going to look closely at why I might not be able to do these things yet. If I could do them, what unimaginable things could I discover within myself, things that perhaps very few have ever had the opportunity to explore?

Meditation

The center located at the base of your spine is felt near the coccyx area. It is the center where fear, as well as the "will to live" develops. A powerful energy lies in wait near this center. When you are at an advanced spiritual level, this energy will become active, rushing up your spine, and circling through the other centers one at a time, fully opening and energizing them before it explodes out the top of your head. When this occurs, you will no longer be chained to the world. Everything then changes. Today, when you are finished with your preliminary exercises, imagine the base of your spine opening and filling with light. Concentrate on the area at the bottom of your spine for a minute before you begin nose tip concentration.

Personal Journal

_____

_____

_____

_____ $\mathcal{D}_{ate}$ _____

DAY 88

Insight

Mountains peek through fleetings of white clouds. Water seeks green valleys below.

Reflections

Today, I think I'll write a poem, but not any poem. This will be a unique style of Japanese poem, a haiku, spiritual in nature with only 17 or 18 syllables. Then, I'll place it in my meditation room.

Meditation

After your preliminary exercises, concentrate a few inches above your head. Do this for about a minute before beginning nose tip concentration. This region above your head is in constant motion, vibrating with intense activity. It is the portal to enlightenment.

Personal Journal

_____
_____
_____
_____ Date _____

DAY 89

Insight

Peak every 18, decline between—the years go by quickly.

Reflections

What existed before time, or thought, or anything else for that matter? Was it a great potentiality consisting of ineffable love and perfect harmony? Was it inconceivable in scope, not subject to laws of physics, perhaps light-years beyond intelligence as I know it? Maybe it wasn't even bound by ideas or logic, and beyond space or universes, beyond conceptualizations. What if this inexplicable love could not contain itself, and flowed out creating the myriad forms that populate the worlds? As a human being, could it be that I eventually developed enough awareness to recognize my separation from this love, this essence of all things from which I have sprung? Can I return to it? If I can somehow harmonize with the singular vibration of this Great Potentiality, will I come face to face with it in this very lifetime? If I can, I'll probably never be able to utter a word about it, but somehow, I'll know.

Meditation

Begin with your three breaths, followed by opening your seven centers. Then practice nose tip concentration. As your mind calms, bodily functions slow as well, with your breathing at times becoming so shallow and refined that the breathing sensation can no longer be felt in the nose. If this happens, your breathing hasn't actually stopped, but your concentration has deepened to the point of not being aware of the feeling of breathing. The tendency is to panic and try to locate the breath again, but this only ruins concentration. Be courageous here; keep your concentration steady. Don't be concerned about breathing or not breathing. Forget about everything including your breathing, and remain in a state of steady concentration.

Personal Journal

_____

_____

_____

_____ Date _____

DAY 90

Insight

Snowflakes! Each so unique in my hand! Oops...they melted.

Reflections

Am I really so different? Doesn't a common denominator weave its way through every one of us, through criminals as well as people like me? What makes us happy, what makes us sad? What satisfies our common thirst? Is it all in some way connected to desire?

Meditation

Maintain nose tip concentration flawlessly. It alone will take you very far. Life will reflect your practice. Life is a mirror or your practice, just as practice is a mirror of your life. You will soon see this for yourself. Whenever you look at your practice, you will see your life. Therefore, if you take each moment of practice, as well as each day of your active life, as the only moment or day that you have, and work within it expecting nothing in return for your labor, just doing what needs ot be done, for yourself and for others, insights will arise.

Personal Journal

_____

_____

_____

_____ Date _____

DAY 91

Insight

Whatever the mind loves...it is only so much.

Reflections

When my perceived reality crumbles, what part of me can stoically observe the devastation? It is not easy to watch my perceptions change, especially treasured perceptions of the many images that have provided my security. It leaves a hole. And although I continue to treasure them, they no longer trick me, which is the one thing that makes it all worthwhile. Because this inquiry into reality has taken root in my heart, I just can't turn my back on my illusions and shrug my shoulders any longer. Little else interests me now, except this marvelous inquiry into reality.

Meditation

At times, you will think that you have fallen asleep during meditation, when actually your mind will be in a state of refined consciousness. Your mind will be aware of subconscious communications from sources unknown, and the exchanges will be very creative. The threshold of slipping in and out of this interesting state is often filled with visions, voices, and involuntary body movements. These are extremely interesting, but if you become involved with them at the expense of your concentration, they will delay deeper insights. These subconscious communications constantly fuel your intuition, not your busybody intellect that definitely will misinterpret them. Normally, however, you are not aware of these hidden connections. These communications are steps toward higher consciousness, but only steps, and nothing with which to become infatuated. This quasi-sleep, however, is a sign that your concentration is becoming calm, and is especially meaningful if accompanied by feelings of merging, unification, or non-dualism. Continue with your nose tip concentration.

Personal Journal

_____

_____

_____

_____ Date _____

Sustained Attention

You have applied your mind to the feeling of the breath inside your nose. Like striking a bell, you have continually applied your mind to this concentration point. One day, however, you will no longer be required to strike that bell, when your mind will strike your concentration object—the feeling of your breath—and your attention will remain there. The bell will then sound continuously. In other words, your attention will remain on the feeling without the interference of disrupting thoughts. At that time, it will be as if the bell tones endlessly without being struck, without effort.

These periods of sustained attention will increase as you progress with your practice. And by averting all the noise of your endless thoughts that have dominated your mind non-stop for all these years, there will be a shift in consciousness. This will lead to other experiences that are quite pleasant, such as constant happiness, but don't become attached to them.

DAY 92

Insight

To kill a living being with glee, such misunderstanding.

Reflections

It is now clear that only a calm, undisturbed mind can plumb the depths required to conquer fear and become free. If I have difficulty reaching these depths, perhaps I should look closely at my life. What am I doing to prolong my own turmoil? Am I insensitive to things, especially the smallest and weakest of creatures?

Meditation

Continue with your nose tip concentration. It is important to strive in perfecting your meditation, but not to strive for results from your practice. Results will take place naturally. Do the exercises completely but not for any particular reason. Ignore what happened during your last session, or what the next session might bring, and even disregard the idea of enlightenment. Resolve to remain with whatever particular day you are on, regardless of how many days that requires, and to do it completely. Don't be worried about the outcome. Consider yourself doing it because it is an opportunity to do something flawlessly, completely, and without expectations of getting something in return. Think about it as a rare opportunity to remain entirely within each moment, moment after moment, with no excess baggage of the past or future.

Personal Journal

_____

_____

_____

_____ Date _____

DAY 93

Insight

I lost my treasure when I stole a penny, doomed my heart when I hurt a friend.

Reflections

I stole something once. I wish I could give it back. I've harmed people psychologically, too. Innocent people. Wouldn't it be nice if I could tell them how sorry I was? These things were done almost unconsciously, as if in a fog of only myself. The sensitive clarity that is beginning to guide my actions now understands...but that doesn't lessen the regrets.

Meditation

Concentration becomes sustained when you stop doubting and fighting your concentration object, and relax into it. Only when you can remain with your breath continuously without distraction will you slip into this refined state of consciousness called "sustained attention." Don't be concerned, however, if sustained attention fails to develop. Our spiritual predispositions vary, and each of us will progress at his or her own pace. Remember always, that although you may feel no progress is being made, sincere meditation, every moment of it, favorably affects your situation in the next world. Continue with your nose tip concentration.

Personal Journal

_____

_____

_____

_____ Date _____

DAY 94

Insight

Lust grows like morning glories in springtime.

Reflections

What do my inappropriate advances and lewd behavior reveal? Wouldn't these kinds of actions reveal a mind that is light-years away from the cool sensitivity required to touch a higher consciousness? Just as an illness slowly eats away at one's heart until nothing is left but a shell, wouldn't the consequences of such reckless actions leave me shipwrecked in my self-made hell where escape is no longer possible?

Meditation

If you are sitting on a cushion, it should be small, quite firm, and placed with only the edge under your tailbone. If you sit in the middle of it, your legs could easily fall asleep. While meditating, if you are continually distracted by a clever mind that can think and count backwards at the same time, then use this complicated counting sequence that forces your mind to pay attention: 1,2,1,2,3,2,1,2,3,4,3,2,1,2,3,4,5,4,3,2,1,etc., up to 10. Then continue with your nose tip concentration.

Personal Journal

_____
_____
_____
_____ _Date_ _____

DAY 95

Insight

The smaller the mind, the larger the lies.

Reflections

Can my meditation deepen without my intentions changing? What results can I expect by forcing my mind to be still during meditation, and then behave recklessly later? My habitual lying and exaggeration reflect a desperate insecurity wherein I attempt to make myself appear better than I actually am. My lying reflects strong desires, where I will do just about anything to get what I want. One power play after the other, trying to control vulnerable, trusting people is another indication of my insecurity. A lying mind will undoubtedly have great difficulty when it confronts the piercing integrity of meditation, so I'm determined to end my lying, not necessarily by trying to stop it, but by admitting to myself all of my insecurities and perceived powerlessness. My lying will only stop when I own up to these things. Then meditation will become effortless, and so will my life.

Meditation

When a toddler first attempts to walk, it falls down repeatedly. Before long, however, it takes a few faltering steps, and soon it is walking. When you try to meditate, you will continuously fall off your concentration object. This falling off and coming back to your concentration object is "striking the bell." At some point, the falling off will stop, and the bell will continue to ring without being struck. This is when your mind can hold the object in concentration continuously without losing it. Then, instead of being a toddler who repeatedly falls down, you become an adult who can walk effortlessly for hours. Continue with your nose tip concentration.

Personal Journal

_____

_____

_____

_____ Date _____

DAY 96

Insight

Only a clear mind penetrates.

Reflections

Using drugs and alcohol as an escape only confuses me and prevents any chance of liberation. How can I expect to see things clearly, in the purity of this precious moment, unless I give up my addictions? Habits are difficult to break, similar to old friends that I simply can't say good-bye to, but I must move beyond them. I can't stay here.

Meditation

Your spiritual mind seeks silence, but because your worldly mind is intimidated by silence and the emptiness of silence, you will find yourself running away from silence in many ways. One is by discussing your spiritual progress. Other than personal questions regarding your practice, it's important to keep your practice to yourself. Spiritual energy dissipates when you talk about your meditation experiences. Eventually, your emptiness must be faced however, so be a hermit during your daily meditations. Then go quietly about your usual business later, but keep your secrets to yourself. Continue with your nose tip concentration.

Personal Journal

_____

_____

_____

_____ *Date* _____

DAY 97

Insight

I'm alone now—with everybody around.

Reflections

Is it possible to ever find truth while I'm busy continually running away from my emptiness? For my entire lifetime I have amused myself—there are endless opportunities—and yet deep inside remains this disquieting, uncomfortable niggle that won't go away.

Meditation

Extend your meditation periods to one hour. At some point, you will surprisingly find yourself remaining on your concentration object for as long as you wish, with no intervening thoughts. When this happens, make sure that you maintain this steadiness for as long as possible. You may exceed one hour if you like at these times, but be careful not to overdo at this stage. It is better to meditate for an hour without fail, twice a day, as your first priority, with an occasional longer period when the mind finds itself going deeply. Have you noticed that at times something other than yourself is in charge of this whole business? Think about attending a retreat center or spending a long weekend at home for extended practice now. Continue with your nose tip concentration.

Personal Journal

_____
_____
_____
_____ Date _____

DAY 98

Insight

Beginnings are priceless, endings divine.

Reflections

I realized today that every victory sows the seeds of defeat, and within every defeat, are the seeds of victory. There are no ultimate winners and losers. This came to me as I noticed how carefully and permanently I cast my heavy footprints in the sand, only to watch them wash away with the tide.

Meditation

The secret is not to strive. Deeper experiences will suddenly occur by themselves—a result of simply being in the moment during meditation, or in life for that matter...you are an impersonal witness to everything. Disturbing thoughts will intervene as you struggle to remain concentrated, but eventually this gives way to an indescribable steadiness. At that time, thinking and scheming unexpectedly stop as your life is changed irrevocably. You don't accomplish this state directly; something just snaps. You might not even be trying to change yourself, or understand anything, it just happens. And when it does, it overwhelms you. Continue with your nose tip concentration.

Personal Journal

_____

_____

_____

_____ Date _____

DAY 99

Insight

The conceit of knowledge, the humility of unknowing.

Reflections

If a single grain of sand symbolizes humankind's accumulated knowledge through the eons, then surely all the sand on all the beaches in all the worlds and in all the universes signifies my spiritual potential beyond knowledge. I search for my true possibilities, my essence.

Meditation

Continue with your beginning exercises, followed by nose tip concentration. Notice the feeling of the in breaths and out breaths, and make certain that your posture is correct. You may spend a few minutes concentrating on any one of your seven centers after your preliminary exercises if you choose to, but remain primarily with the feeling of your breath as a concentration object. The feeling of the breath is a unique focusing object. It brings up deepening experiences, the first of which is the ability to remain concentrated on the feeling of the breath without continually losing attention. Instead of striking the bell time after time, the bell continues to ring on its own. This is a big step. Just remain with your continuous, intense awareness, and soon deeper experiences will occur. Be alert now for any attempt by your mind to distract you from meditation. There might be a compulsion to do something, perhaps go somewhere else to meditate, write a book, begin your own meditation group, and so forth. If you can resist these impulses, seeing them all as ruses by the mind to disturb your meditation, you will now go deeper. You might also feel listless and hopeless before this deepening occurs, but this is only temporary. These types of negative feelings and doubt many times forecast a deepening.

Personal Journal 🌸

_____
_____
_____
_____ *Date* _____

DAY 100

Insight

High mountains, blue sky, open heart.

Reflections

My mind's suggestive powers are amazing. They compel me to do so many things, all so exciting and necessary. The myriad thoughts begin as tiny sparks that blaze into the bonfires that destroy me. I can see that only in the absence of thought, in this one precious moment, can I touch my deepest being. But my mind constantly attempts to remember this moment; it tries to hold it, possess it, analyze it, and sort it out. Tragically, the truth of my moment then disappears, replaced only by my confused interpretation of it. You see, while I was busy remembering the last moment, the truth of the present moment slipped by, unnoticed, and I completely missed it. And now, sadly, I realize that I have completely missed the truth of life as well.

Meditation

Meditation becomes effortless when virtue arises, and virtue arises because of meditation. Meditation and virtue work hand-in-hand. As you become increasingly mindful due to the influence of meditation, non-virtuous activity will become more painfully apparent in both yourself and others. This seeing, alone, without any particular attempt to change yourself, will alter your activities. It changes the underlying consciousness in your mind that creates feelings and emotions, which in turn produce thought patterns. Stay true to your nose tip concentration, beginning every session with your preliminary exercises.

Personal Journal

_____

_____

_____

_____ Date _____

DAY 101

Insight

No shortcut to eternity.

Reflections

This is difficult work, this meditation. It involves watching my mind. This work is internal, not external such as the activity in the world where my mind rules. Somebody not acquainted with meditation might suppose that I am wasting my time, sitting on the floor and doing nothing, but internally, I am deepening myself spiritually, preparing to move past the uncertainty of this human condition. The work is difficult, I understand this, but I also know that if I do it properly, and for some time, it will lead me toward enlightenment.

Meditation

At some point in your practice, don't be surprised if you experience particularly strong emotions, when you might cry or laugh, or do both at the same time. This is a phase through which to work. It's okay; you might have touched the primal bliss buried deep in your consciousness, or uncovered things you might have been repressing, perhaps old emotions that are being hung out to dry. As you become sensitive to your mind, things will come up that may have been brushed aside or justified in the past. At times, the intense joy of spiritual release, which is felt but not always understood, will appear as "happy attacks" as well. These can occur at random and for no apparent reason, when our eyes suddenly fill with tears, and we're not sure if we are about to laugh or cry. It is actually neither of these emotions; it's a tremendous relief. Continue with your nose tip concentration.

Personal Journal

_____

_____

_____

_____ *Date* _____

A Year to Enlightenment

DAY 102

Insight

Float downstream; paddle furiously upstream. Any difference?

Reflections

I look at what I want in this world, and the tremendous effort that's involved in getting it. In the end, I want happiness, like everybody else, but the question is, what will really make me happy, and what will only imprison me further? Determining this certainly requires wisdom.

Meditation

When you reach a point at which your mind remains concentrated with few disruptions, you might discover that your lifestyle is affecting the quality of your meditation. Experiment with a few things, such as where you are living, your leisure activities, perhaps your work environment or diet. Notice how you speak to others and your normal topics of conversation. Who are your friends? Whom do you relate to and emulate? Are you overly concerned about your body or physical appearance, or if you are striving too hard or too little? These and many other things can affect your concentration, but no real guidelines exist, other than discovering in your heart what's best. Just observe clearly and carefully, being completely honest with yourself regarding your intentions. Try to be aware of how you feel when you don't get what you want, how you react to that feeling, and what you believe to be the entity that is experiencing all of this. You can never be lazy about these inquiries. Continue with your nose tip concentration.

Personal Journal

_____

_____

_____

_____ Date _____

DAY 103

Insight

Old habits die hard.

Reflections

When I restrain myself by quietly practicing meditation, it can be frustrating. There are many other interesting things to do rather than sitting here feeling bored. I could be having fun going here and there with my friends, and the practice seems to be an unnecessary bother. What makes it more difficult is that nothing seems to be happening and it is just plain, old, hard work. The temptation is always there for me to do something else. The world has dominated my mind for so long that my habit patterns are entrenched. They won't surrender quietly or depart without a fight, digging in hard since the initial exuberance of this new meditation experiment wore off. But having admitted all of this, I also know that there is no escape from the reality of humankind's trials and tribulations, so the sooner I face it, the sooner I will free myself.

Meditation

Meditate as usual, and as you watch your thoughts arise and float away, determine if these thoughts are the sum and substance of your being. If not, what is behind the thoughts? Anything? Is there a watcher? Or is the watcher merely a memory of the last thought...just another thought? Does one "thought moment" cause the next, ad infinitum, or is there something much deeper, something beyond that surface watcher, something that "knows," something that you haven't touched yet? Continue with your nose tip concentration.

Personal Journal

_____

_____

_____

_____ Date _____

DAY 104

Insight

Fear knows not the moment.

Reflections

I'm frightened by tomorrow. I could become ill, have an accident of some kind, or run into some bad luck...maybe lose my job. I seem to be whistling in the dark while at the same time subconsciously projecting troubling possibilities into my future. What if I could leave all of that behind and live completely in the moment, that mystical place that can't be touched by unpleasant memories or future calamities? Where could fear possibly find a toehold here?

Meditation

Continue with your practice. Stay keenly concentrated on the feeling of your breath as it touches the inside of your nose and floods your body. Keep your focus intense and remain completely within each moment. When you walk or cycle outdoors, allow no thoughts to intervene, just observe and remain aware of your breath at all times. This will take serious practice. You won't be meditating on your nose, you will be meditating on every sense stimulation that arises—sights, smells, sounds—but instead of concentrating on them, you must release them as soon as they contact your mind, as if they are thoughts. Be in nature, but don't become lost in it.

Personal Journal

_____
_____
_____
_____ _Date_ _____

DAY 105

Insight

False courtesy betrays us both.

Reflections

It is very dishonest when I pretend—making believe that I'm something I'm not, or acting in certain ways to get attention (my little poses, my witty retorts, my staged personality). Why am I afraid to be myself, regardless of how awful that might be? It doesn't seem proper to mislead others just because I'm such a coward to be me; it's a subtle form of lying. If I'm true to myself, being exactly who I am, at least I could see what I have to work with. I guess this is where I have to begin if I truly want to change, by honestly stopping and looking at myself. The only problem is, if I stop lying to myself, I have no choice but to become responsible!

Meditation

Always remain relaxed during meditation. If you experience any heart problems—palpitations or pressure in your chest—this is a sure sign of stress and indicates that you are doing something wrong. Immediately stop concentrating and relax your whole body with each breath. Then, when you do return to concentration, be certain to take this relaxation into your practice. It is more of a watching with bright anticipation than a striving to get somewhere, as if you are waiting for a beautiful sunrise without trying to push the sun up. Never push, never strive, because it simply doesn't work. Yes, you might push yourself into some kind of realization, but it will be a shallow, self-imposed one. All you're doing is adding more bricks to a structure that must be eventually dismantled. Continue with your nose tip concentration.

Personal Journal

_____

_____

_____

_____ Date _____

A Year to Enlightenment

DAY 106

Insight

All that is built will crumble. Build not.

Reflections

Isn't it more of a dissolution than a construction, this spiritual enlightenment? Everything I gather to myself seems to be subject to loss, so the answer can only be in not accumulating. Is this the secret of meditation? Nothing gained? How will I ever get anywhere if I don't gain something?

Meditation

Simply remain with the feeling of your breath with no ambition other than that. Then results, like unconditional love, will come along by themselves. Continue with your nose tip concentration. Walk or cycle outdoors as much as possible, playing "touch and go" with all that encounters your mind.

Personal Journal

_____

_____

_____

_____ _Date_ _____

DAY 107

Insight

Today, be alive! Celebrate! Be free!

Reflections

I'm beginning to think that worrying about tomorrow is just plain dumb. It's a lack of insight, not understanding that everything is my teacher. Of course, I have to buy a few groceries and pay the rent, that's a responsibility and a reality of living in the world, but to worry constantly about anything beyond this...wouldn't that keep me from freedom?

Meditation

At this stage of meditation where you can remain concentrated on your object, a common mistake is to think, I am staying with my object! This, of course, is a thought. It takes you off your meditation object by thinking. Thoughts can be very subtle, wisps of images in the mind, so be alert as you continue to deepen your practice. Don't forget to keep your shoulders and face relaxed, and to breathe as instructed. If you find your body tightening up in meditation, look into your daily life and see where the tightening occurs there as well. Continue with your nose tip concentration.

Personal Journal

_____

_____

_____

_____ Date _____

DAY 108

Insight

You are exactly where you need to be.

Reflections

Aren't there still lessons for me to learn? Perhaps no matter where I find myself, that is the exact place for my next discovery. Adverse situations, of course, always seem to diminish my opportunities, but perhaps they actually enhance them. Adversity forces me to learn something about myself. What exactly is an adverse situation? I suppose that an adverse situation is something opposed to what I want, but do I really know what's good for me? Maybe no situation is adverse.

Meditation

There is nothing in meditation for your mind to learn, so the pressure is off. Just watch your breath, day after day, and trust that freedom is close. Stay relaxed and focused. Establish your concentration, then set it on autopilot and watch keenly. Continue with your nose tip concentration. Meditation itself will take care of everything.

Personal Journal

_____

_____

_____

_____ *Date* _____

DAY 109

Insight

Faith, effort, mindfulness, concentration, and wisdom. A balancing act!

Reflections

Experiencing for myself that I am changing and that meditation is leading toward freedom is my basis of faith. Accompanying this increasing faith is the realization that a strong, strenuous, but relaxed effort is required—and that a certain kind of mindfulness must be maintained. There is no doubt that deep concentration must be cultivated if the resulting wisdom I seek will someday be strong.

Meditation

Your areas of concentration will be devoted to three types of objects: material, fine material, and immaterial. These are things that make up your familiar worlds—worlds that are, regrettably, all subject to disintegration. Beyond these three types of objects are mysterious areas neither associated in any way with worlds that fall apart, nor able to be known intellectually. Although these areas beyond are incomprehensible to your mind, they can be known intuitively, and reaching them will be a direct result of your efforts that must be grounded in material, fine material, and immaterial concentration. The only requirement is your effort at this time—in these worlds with which you are familiar. Continue with your nose tip concentration.

Personal Journal

_____

_____

_____

_____ Date _____

DAY 110

Insight

Men ferociously defend their beliefs, for soon, it is all they have left.

Reflections

It is apparent that my faith must be balanced with my wisdom. If my faith is weak and my wisdom powerful, I'll surely analyze my practice to death and impede my concentration. However, if my wisdom is weak and my faith too strong, I'll surely lack discrimination, believing anything that I'm told without proving it true for myself. I could find myself wandering down paths that will lead to delusion instead of insight and the freedom of unconditional love.

Meditation

For some, insight arrives quickly. For others, slowly. Nothing can be rushed nor can you compare yourself to others in these spiritual pursuits. Because our spiritual inclinations are different, it is common for a novice meditator to be far advanced compared to someone who has been meditating for years. Conscientiously, do your own work and everything will fall into place. Never worry about your progress or try to compete with others, for progress is usually made without your being aware of it. Suddenly, one day, an insight will flash and you will wonder where it came from. It came from your diligent practice. On the days when your practice is terrible, when you can barely stand to meditate, these are the days when you are extremely productive. Continue with your nose tip concentration.

Personal Journal

_____
_____
_____
_____ Date _____

DAY III

Insight

Work not for results.

Reflections

My concentration must balance my effort. When my effort is strong but I can't seem to concentrate, my mind becomes restless and distracted, but when my concentration is so strong that I lose awareness, my mind falls into trance states and I become lax and dull. This is when walking meditation becomes invaluable.

Meditation

Supernormal understanding only comes about when virtue takes hold. Virtue calms your mind from its frenzied activities so that sustained concentration can develop. Real virtue is a direct result of your ability to see non-virtuous behavior, and as such, both virtue and concentration walk together supporting each other. Simply be continuously aware of everything, not only your breath in meditation but also your actions, and especially your speech. Everything will take care of itself then, with only your undivided attention being the effort required. Continue with your nose tip concentration.

Personal Journal

_____

_____

_____

_____ Date _____

DAY 112

Insight

Watch everything as you watch waves lapping white sands—for no particular reason.

Reflections

I have seen in my practice that faith, effort, concentration, and wisdom must balance each other. But mindfulness is the exception. Mindfulness needs no balancing at all. My only requirement is to make certain that mindfulness is constant, powerful, and uninterrupted during meditation...maybe this is true of life as well.

Meditation

For today's sessions, simply sit, with no particular exercises—no special breathing, no concentration—just remain keenly aware of whatever enters your consciousness. Physical feelings, thoughts, emotions—be mindful of every little ripple, but don't swirl around with them. These emotional feelings might come up as subtle levels of doubt accompanied by a lack of conviction or trust. Sensual desires might arise in the form of lust, or the feelings might reflect an underlying discontent, a laziness or lackadaisical effort, or perhaps even distraction, worry, anger, and aversion. Watch all of this carefully. Initially, you might not feel like sitting at all, preferring to go to bed, read, or watch TV. You might feel restless and tired, perhaps doubting that meditation is worth all the effort, and later, when your sitting position becomes uncomfortable, you might want to frequently change your position. Then, if you continue to resist moving, the desire to replace the uncomfortable sensation with one of relief could build and eventually turn into anger. All of these types of subtle feelings should be considered only arising and passing phenomena as you continue quietly sitting. These are the same feelings you face every day when life becomes unpleasant.

Personal Journal

_____
_____
_____
_____ *Date* _____

DAY 113

Insight

A life of labor results from compromising our true passion.

Reflections

A subtle sensitivity and intelligence is developing. As I advance in my practice, I realize that this same sensitivity and intelligence builds the foundation from which every virtue arises. Now, when I see the beauty of the forest or the beauty of a human being, there is no compelling urge to acquire them. Wisdom prevails, as everything is seen in its natural beauty and wonder, without desire, and my every action is exquisitely honorable. The unity of the universe is becoming apparent, where everything is protected within an envelope of immense love and compassion. Someday, I'll discover what it is I love to do. Then, I will tap into unlimited energy that will be used, hand-in-hand along with my innate abilities, to help raise the consciousness of all beings.

Meditation

Return to your regular nose tip concentration. Let nothing disturb your practice as you dedicate yourself fully and single-mindedly. See thoughts with a loving indifference, as a witness and not a participant. Have no doubt about what you are doing, and surrender to this moment, moving subtly within its currents.

Personal Journal

_____

_____

_____

_____ *Date* _____

DAY 114

Insight

Tears streaming down her face, she looked toward the heavens for help.

Reflections

It is difficult for me to ask for help, much easier to give it. Why is this? Am I afraid of appearing susceptible? Has the wall that I have built around myself for security only imprisoned me? Can I ever truly love without first becoming vulnerable?

Meditation

When thoughts no longer come between you and your meditation, you will find yourself absorbing into your concentration object. This absorption, a steady focus similar to the constant after-tone of a bell rather than the sound of it just being struck, now lays the groundwork for other possibilities. Strive for nothing in meditation; allow it to happen by itself. The only effort required is a focusing of the mind, and even that effort becomes tranquil after the mind sustains a focused awareness. Then there is only an abiding in this moment. Continue with your nose tip concentration.

Personal Journal

_____

_____

_____

_____ Date _____

DAY 115

Insight

Live simply. Somewhere between need and greed lie the killing fields of war.

Reflections

When I accumulate more than I need, dishonesty creeps into my life like a thief in the night.

Meditation

When the merging with your meditation object becomes sustainable, a sense of relief blankets your mind like a cool day after a long, hot summer. If other feelings and sensations arise as well, notice them as you notice your thoughts before releasing them. Otherwise, distractions will block what is coming next, which will definitely have a much greater impact. Continue with your nose tip concentration.

Personal Journal

_____
_____
_____
_____ Date _____

DAY 116

Insight

Round and round we go, when we stop, then we know.

Reflections

My mind secretly fears meditation. It instinctively knows that this inner reflection will question its authority. That's why I initially hesitated to begin this practice; I wasn't ready to risk trading control for an outside chance that meditation will someday alter my destiny forever. I wanted a contract, a sure-clad agreement before beginning something like this. Sadly, back then, taking just a few minutes out of my frantic routine was asking far too much of me, as I rushed around and around on my never-ending carousel of illusions, spending my entire lifetime accumulating wealth and experiences that I can only borrow for the short time I am here.

Meditation

Continue with your regular practice, being careful not to modify it in any way. Experiences or whispered suggestions encountered in meditation could very well be the untrusting mind trying to regain control. If the suggestions are authentic supernormal communications, the mind will surely misinterpret them at this stage, and ignoring them will not diminish their ultimate effects. Continue with your nose tip concentration.

Personal Journal

_____

_____

_____

_____ Date _____

DAY 117

Insight

Enlightenment unfolds.

Reflections

Meditation appears to be a state of not knowing, and when I'm in this state of not knowing, the self that I believe in so passionately is absent in some way. This is when I surely make my best progress toward enlightenment. Conversely, when I think that I know something and securely store the information in my mind, my self is alive and well. These storage files are where accumulated memories and knowledge linger, and where enlightenment can never be found. I know where enlightenment is now—it is in this immense moment where my self can never tread.

Meditation

After periods of sustained concentration, with thoughts relatively absent, certain sensations can come up; one is unprovoked happiness. You might break out in a broad smile and wonder where this seemingly marvelous happy attack came from. Don't concern yourself; these things are only markers on the road for you to enjoy for the moment. If you dawdle at these little scenic spots, it will delay your journey; smell the flowers, but continue on! Maintain your nose tip concentration.

Personal Journal

_____

_____

_____

_____ _Date_ _____

DAY 118

Insight

Why live behind dark curtains?

Reflections

What is it that keeps me from freedom? Not conventional freedom, such as traveling the world or doing as I please, but freedom from myself? My bondage seems connected to a mysterious responsibility. If I truly had nothing left to lose, wouldn't having nothing left to lose be liberating? What exactly am I terrified of losing? If only I could mystically exchange my feelings of emotional attachment for compassionate indifference. What would happen then?

Meditation

A thought that interrupts your concentration could be something visual, such as a picture of yourself, or verbal chatter. A loving embrace of the thought, always within your mindfulness and allowing it to pass through, is the course of action, never a disdainful pushing away. It is natural for your mind to think, just don't attach and glue yourself to any particular thought, either visual or verbal. Stay aloof with an affectionate detachment. Continue with your nose tip concentration.

Personal Journal

_____

_____

_____

_____ Date _____

DAY 119

Insight

A failed spiritual life—only because of careless words.

Reflections

After encountering my first true taste of spirituality, I find myself naturally setting new priorities in my life. Every spiritual advance seems to require a worldly sacrifice; that's just the way it seems to be, but my sacrifices are involuntary. Good examples are my speech and sexual habits. I just watch them. I don't do anything ascetic. I'm simply aware that I'm going to speak before I speak, and in the same way anticipate my sexual activities. I'm not judging anything or radically changing my behavior. Patience is required here because my mind wants to charge ahead and make premature changes, but that's not necessary; these close observations themselves are leaving me with no alternative but to change.

Meditation

For today's sessions only, anticipate each in breath and out breath before they are taken. As you are breathing in, anticipate breathing out. As you are breathing out, anticipate breathing in. Don't control your breathing, however. Breathe naturally. Likewise, before you speak, be aware that you are going to speak, then closely watch what is said. Your speech reveals the contents of your mind and the depth of your understanding.

Personal Journal

_____

_____

_____

_____ Date _____

DAY 120

Insight

Between the peaceful valleys of compassion and the lofty peaks of wisdom, lie insights.

Reflections

When I overreact, I simply do more than necessary to handle a situation. When I underreact, I avoid the situation. Harmony occurs when I tackle a situation, but only do what's necessary to resolve things. This falls somewhere in between under- and overreaction. When confronted with circumstances, do I look into the heart of them? Do I really make an effort to move my opinions and myself aside for a moment before I act, so that I can get to the root of the problem? Wouldn't the resulting action be decisive and intelligent? But if I act before seeing the circumstances in their entirety, then the consequences of my hasty actions could be endless.

Meditation

When you notice thoughts interrupting your practice, try not to overreact by aggressively cutting them off—or under react by allowing them to continue. Take an approach that's not very exciting but insightful: Just watch your thoughts. This innocent watching makes them quite uncomfortable and soon they will be on their way. Continue with your nose tip concentration.

Personal Journal 🪷

_____

_____

_____

_____ _Date_ _____

DAY 121

Insight

Step by step, vulnerable and trusting.

Reflections

I keep alert for any strange or unusual occurrences during practice, anything connected subtly to my breath, or connected to feelings, emotions, or sensations. I also take note of any visions, ideas, or imaginations. After practice, I watch for any insights that might arise connected with my regular daily routine; perhaps a new way to do something, a new way of looking at something—any kind of little revelation.

Meditation

Particularly watch the visual thoughts appearing in your mind—a picture of your body or a picture of your face. These pictures are thoughts, too; thoughts that quickly become a watcher creating further story lines with interesting dialogues. Then the story lines invariably cascade into great dramas. Keep returning to your breath until you can remain there effortlessly. Continue with your nose tip concentration.

Personal Journal

_____

_____

_____

_____ Date _____

DAY 122

Insight

The mind begs for sanctuary.

Reflections

How can I find peace within a mind that's always in turmoil and wants constantly to control things? How can I get beyond this ongoing confusion and find that something? It's obvious that the first step is to observe this mind objectively until I know everything about it. How else will its mystique be resolved? Maybe only then can I use it exclusively for its limited purposes in the world, where it is most effective and comfortable, instead of letting its illusions infringe on that deep level of my being where spirituality is to be found.

Meditation

By watching thoughts day by day, you become acquainted with your mind. Have you discovered its secrets yet? Its masterful deceptions? Continue with nose tip concentration.

Personal Journal

_____

_____

_____

_____ *Date* _____

Physical Happiness

Are you increasingly able to keep your concentration steady without intervening thoughts? Can you keep the bell ringing without having to strike it? When you can, don't be surprised if physical feelings of exquisite happiness and rapture wash over you, so powerful that the hair on your arms and on the back of your neck stands on end as if you have seen something supernatural. Again, be careful of becoming enamored with these or any other feelings. Just enjoy them for the moment and then gently ease them from your memory, preparing yourself for what's coming next. This happiness, as well as many things described in this book, will not occur with all meditators. More often than not, unusual experiences will not occur at all, until suddenly, one day, the meditator understands.

DAY 123

Insight

Security. The world's greatest myth.

Reflections

Illusions of perceived security filled my mind at one time. This has changed because I no longer see my mind as the principle mover of my being. The option I once had of choosing between perceived security and insight is now gone. All that remains is for me to trust my practice.

Meditation

Continue with your nose tip concentration.

Personal Journal

_____
_____
_____
_____ $\mathcal{D}_{ate}$ _____

DAY 124

Insight

Five barriers block the path.

Reflections

Craving for the things that I think will brighten my life, being hostile toward others, being lethargic and not caring, worrying, being distracted, being cynical, lacking conviction and trust—these all burden my life. But which one of these dominates my life? I must find out. When I do, I won't necessarily suppress it, but will embrace it as a fact and go from there. If I suppress it, it will forever haunt me. I'm determined to get to the root of these things by keeping them visible and out in the open, observing them very carefully until I'm finished with them.

Meditation

Thoughts repeatedly cycle in predictable patterns. Notice these developing patterns carefully during your practice because they are indicators pointing toward your freedom. Remember to remain relaxed in your practice as you continue with your nose tip concentration.

Personal Journal

_____
_____
_____
_____ Date _____

DAY 125

Insight

You are never angry; anger is you.

Reflections

I'm learning to just observe my anger now. I allow it to arise, feeling its physical presence—the rising blood pressure, the flurry of thoughts, and the extreme desire to dominate and take control. I carefully observe its results, too—how it tires my heart and remains with me long after the incident is over, how it affects not only me, but everybody around me. Anger is what I am in those unfortunate moments. There it is, the anger, it cannot be denied. I'm only deceiving myself if I think that I am something other than that.

Meditation

During meditation, simply watch the feeling of the breath throughout the body...over and over. See what develops. You are learning to observe, beginning with your breath and then with your thoughts. Whatever you experience in practice is taken into life, so you will learn to observe your emotions as well. Continue with nose tip concentration.

Personal Journal

_____

_____

_____

_____ *Date* _____

DAY 126

Insight

Tuck your impatience into the pocket of acceptance.

Reflections

When I push too hard, things don't take their natural course. They go awry and are never done well, becoming easily undone. Waiting patiently for the right moment to act and then knowing intuitively what to do must require a tremendous amount of insight.

Meditation

Don't hurry things. Just watch, wait, and observe the feeling of your breath. Continue with nose tip concentration.

Personal Journal

_____
_____
_____
_____ Date _____

DAY 127

Floating

Merely direct your mind to your concentration point. This is the extent of your responsibilities. The practice will take care of everything else. The energy that results from this could take many forms, for example, a floating sensation, or a lightening flash feeling of rapture. Stay within your concentration when and if these happen. The sensations are pleasant if they occur, but are only temporary respites on your journey, and doesn't necessarily happen to all meditators.

Insight

Minds lacking momentary awareness are controlled by laziness.

Reflections

Tremendous energy is required to accomplish things. Can that energy be tapped without the desire to accomplish? What would be the result of undirected, unlimited energy? Perhaps something unimaginable, such as the birth of a universe!

Meditation

Continue with your nose tip concentration.

Personal Journal

_____

_____

_____

_____ *Date* _____

DAY 128

Insight

Doubt everything until you prove it true for yourself.

Reflections

When I'm skeptical, isn't my mind protecting me? But when I see the truth and still have doubts, is my mind then protecting itself? I'm beginning to understand these things from different perspectives now, perspectives of indifferent awareness rather than those of personal involvement.

Meditation

Continue with nose tip concentration. Remember your preliminary exercises.

Personal Journal

_____

_____

_____

_____ Date _____

DAY 129

Insight

Wanting: The scourge of humankind.

Reflections

How many countless conflicts have I caused others and myself by impulsively wanting things I don't have, or trying to rid myself of annoyances? Aren't these the root causes of my discontent—this constant craving and wanting? How can I ever hope to become internally integrated if I am constantly torn by these incessant desires? I seem to be bent forward constantly, always inclining toward something.

Meditation

When you enter your meditation area, leave all ambitions behind. Don't attempt to create an experience or develop wisdom. Don't even try to change your life. Only watch the feeling of your breath throughout the body and the inside of your nose. It is very simple. Be patient. Know that meditation will accomplish everything by itself. Don't allow your mind to interfere. Be cautious, however, for the deeper you go, the more your mind will attempt to distract you. With your first, fleeting taste of freedom, life might acquire an exquisitely delicious flavor and distractions could become irresistible. Continue with your nose tip concentration.

Personal Journal

_____

_____

_____

_____ $Date$ _____

DAY 130

Insight

If you seek holiness, don't live with thieves.

Reflections

My associates and my activities do affect my practice. At some point, when I'm stronger perhaps, associations won't influence me, but for my blossoming heart, they can be worrisome at times.

Meditation

If you can arrange your schedule, attend a retreat center. Take this time off to devote yourself strictly to practice. Legitimate centers are resident communities of dedicated people who have been meditating regularly for many years, and who will be genuinely interested in your spiritual development. They won't charge fees or solicit donations, trusting that their costs will somehow be covered, and are grateful for whatever contributions, be it money or work, which you might volunteer. They will be quiet and peacefully gentle, but exacting regarding adherence to their schedule and appropriate behavior. There will be no surprises or attempts to influence you with their particular beliefs. Always use wisdom and be alert when choosing a meditation center. The initial feeling you might have about a center should always be confirmed with your actual experience of it. Continue with your nose tip concentration.

Personal Journal

_____

_____

_____

_____ _Date_ _____

DAY 131

Insight

SELF expression, amazing; self-expression, distasteful.

Reflections

I must begin to see and feel with my heart and not with my head. This involves a significant transformation. If I refuse to make this dramatic change, and instead continue to escape into my frantic activities, then I'll remain trapped in my state of confusion—at least until I'm shaken to the core someday when my illusions are shattered. I know there is no escape. I recognize that I must somehow make an effort to see. Only with vision does the real possibility of freedom exist—not the freedom to do as I please, but the freedom to be truly what I am, and not what I think that I should become.

Meditation

Surprising or unusual things can appear during nose tip concentration. Notice them, but immediately return to your concentration. Never anticipate these things. Sit quietly, keep your mind unmoving and focused, and this alone will take you to many places, including your goal. Continue with your nose tip concentration, always beginning with your three circling breaths and your energy center exercise.

Personal Journal

_____
_____
_____
_____ *Date* _____

DAY 132

Insight

Silence—the sound of eternity.

Reflections

In order to see, I must remain quiet. I must calm my busy mind so that intuitive communications can penetrate my opening heart. These voices are so fragile. They are astonishing, loving whispers barely distinguishable above the stillness. Therefore, for only a moment, I will forsake my ambitions.

Meditation

Now use the counting technique, backwards from 100 to check your concentration—one count with each out breath. If you lose count, start again from the beginning. Don't encourage feelings or sensations—the fewer experiences the better. Excitement only delays insight. Whatever arises, delight in it for the moment but don't hold on to it. After the counting exercise, continue with nose tip concentration.

Personal Journal

_____

_____

_____

_____ *Date* _____

DAY 133

Insight

Originally, it was one. Still is, actually!

Reflections

Supernormal communications seem to vibrate at a deep, singular intensity, while my everyday thoughts and emotions vibrate feebly at shallow, frenzied levels. Only when these weaker intensities of my thoughts and emotions subside during meditation do I approach that powerful, steady, unified pulsation. Slowly, ever so slowly, I am moving from my head to my heart—from the choppy, surface waves of the storm to the quiet, calm depths of the sea.

Meditation

At times during meditation, you might experience fearful, reoccurring feelings and thoughts; an example might be impending death. This is quite common. When this occurs, merely consider them to be arising and passing thoughts and feelings, and release them quickly. Take shelter in your meditation object. Continue with your nose tip concentration.

Personal Journal

_____
_____
_____
_____ *Date* _____

DAY 134

Insight

Not always a pleasant solution, but a permanent one—this meditation.

Reflections

Something unusual happens when I approach the singular wisdom of my Source—my life becomes dramatically less stressful. For some mysterious reason, I find myself naturally limiting my choices and simplifying things. This simplification doesn't result from thinking how to simplify; it is an indirect result of meditation. This simplification is difficult to explain, but once insight and wisdom stir within me, the allure of the world and its millions of things begins to slip away involuntarily. I might occasionally revisit something, hoping to recapture that old feeling, but each visit results in disappointment, with my lack of interest confirmed. I feel like a kid who has lost interest in her dolls, outgrowing them but still displaying them on her bed. Something else is attracting me now, the one instead of the many. It is so wonderful, so frightening.

Meditation

Continue with your nose tip concentration. Be careful not to create images in your mind of the nose tip. Feel the breath on it each time, as if for the first time. Also, peripherally notice the incoming and outgoing breath every time as they flood the body. Extend the out breath two or three times longer than the in breath, and notice the subtle hesitation between the in and out breath. Concentrate as if the feeling of each breath is the first time you have ever experienced it.

Personal Journal

_____

_____

_____

_____ *Date* _____

A Year to Enlightenment

DAY 135

Waves of Joy

By now, you might have experienced some unexpected benefits from practice. Trust that this is only the beginning, and it all starts with your preliminary exercises and your concentration. At this point, you might experience some other things, such as waves of incredible joy washing over your entire body or joy filling and suffusing your body. Enjoy this if it happens, but don't attempt to repeat it. Simply continue with your practice and be prepared for whatever comes next.

Insight

Overflowing the mind door/A flood of thoughts create/ A selfhood quite unique we think/And here we doom our fate.

Reflections

I am a master of escapes. I can pull off simple ones, such as losing myself in a good book , or complex ones in which I surrender myself to someone or some cause completely, willing to sacrifice my life for them. Within these precious moments, worries about me are gone. Could that kind of psychological release become permanent, without the uncertainty of a tenuous relationship or a fleeting cause? Could I prove in my heart that my self really doesn't exist? If so, couldn't I then release this self forever, freeing myself from a great burden? The alternative is to remain anchored in this self, where instead of a release, I can only look forward to eternal incarceration.

Meditation

Continue with nose tip concentration. It should be obvious soon that meditation is something you can rely on, even in dire circumstances.

Personal Journal

_____

_____

_____

_____ Date _____

DAY 136

Insight

The world of man is lust, leading to possessiveness, leading to killing. And so it is.

Reflections

My body is made of chemicals. A certain combination of these chemicals produces hunger, while other combinations create lust, anger, and depression. It's not complicated—even I can understand this. My "I" thought, or self, is created in my brain from chemical activity as well, and acts as a bodyguard. The big problem I have with this self or "I" thought is that maybe it is merely chemical reactions producing a memory—and how can memory effectively deal with what's happening right now? How can I ever be spontaneous and insightful when I act only from my dead, past experiences? Is this why I act so dimwittedly? No wonder I'm stuck!

Meditation

Valuable progress occurs when seemingly no progress is being made, so remain true to your opening exercises and nose tip concentration. Go back and verify that you haven't become careless and altered the process. The human condition must be clearly seen, because an awareness of these circumstances is what ignites the fuse toward enlightenment.

Personal Journal 🪷

_____

_____

_____

_____ Date _____

A Year to Enlightenment

DAY 137

Insight

For what do we save ourselves?

Reflections

I think that this road to enlightenment must be traveled in the same manner that a tree gracefully bows to the wind. I have relied upon my cunning logic heavily in the past and this has only delayed progress. They say the answer is deep inside, guarded by 10 great difficulties. This I believe is true, and I believe that the least of these difficulties must be strong doubt. I am so skeptical of anything not immediately obvious to my physical senses, which includes the mind. It is difficult to break down these stubborn obstacles, these barriers in myself that refuse to consider possibilities beyond my limited vision. Meditation is helping.

Meditation

At times, your practice will be filled with nos. Thoughts come in—No! You feel like moving—No! You would rather watch TV—No! Someday, however, there will be a resounding "Yes!" when all objections fall away and you become one with, and surrender to, your practice. Then, you will no longer be required to carry water up a steep hill to your garden. You'll contentedly sit under blossoming apple trees while the heavens shower you. Continue with your nose tip concentration.

Personal Journal

_____

_____

_____

_____ Date _____

DAY 138

Insight

Become nothing, no different from the fleeting breath. There! You're gone!

Reflections

Doesn't my heart have to break? It is so rigid. Mustn't it painfully break open, like a husk, so that the seed inside can grow? What choice do I have but to accept the pain and disappointment—the emptiness—by saying no to my desires, until that day when wisdom arises? When that day finally comes, will my fleeting, feeble attempts to escape give way to unconditional love? And then, will my heart open forever? What else can I do?

Meditation

Stay with your breath, hour after hour, day after day. Be patient, be alert, and be especially compassionate toward yourself. Always keep in mind what it is that you are trying to accomplish—your goal of freedom. It is not too far away. Continue with your nose tip concentration.

Personal Journal

_____
_____
_____
_____ Date _____

DAY 139

Insight

Roads leading nowhere.

Reflections

Can I really risk everything? When I own something, could it be that I am the one possessed? Is it possible that as soon as I release it, it magically flies back into my arms in a different form, recreated, offering me unlimited freedom?

Meditation

As your mind now remains focused with increasingly bright, aware anticipation, and with few interruptions, a certain type of rapture might arise in which your body becomes flooded, then bursts with joy. This could occur at any time, either during or after meditation. Again, delight in the experience, but let it go. Don't become attached to it or attempt to repeat it. Your mind will take any experience resulting from meditation and try to use it for its own purposes in your daily life, and once the mind becomes involved, everything is skewed. This is because the mind misinterprets things, and the results are never good. This mental imaging only impedes your progress, so maintain your diligent awareness at all times. Continue with your nose tip concentration.

Personal Journal

_____

_____

_____

_____ Date _____

DAY 140

Insight

Light cannot be seen, but it exists...witnessed by its reflections.

Reflections

My emotions are slowly being altered by my spiritual essence, although it is difficult to explain how they've changed. While my mind mimics what it is like to be holy, my intuition actually creates those circumstances within me. Surrender, not control, is the inevitable answer.

Meditation

Don't manage your practice. Follow your guide and things will progress. Be wary of the mind, for it will constantly try to take control. It understands nothing of spirit but tricks you into believing that it does. Continue with your nose tip concentration. Those with strong personalities based on illusionary "I" thoughts usually have difficulty sitting in meditation, and later have trouble going deeply into concentration because without action, the "I" begins to dissolve. Without constant attachment and clinging, which some call love—and without aversion, which include anger and hatred—maintaining the image of a self or an "I" thought is difficult. The more "love" and hatred we feel, the more alive we feel. All of this is connected to wanting, and it is only when we stop wanting that the "I" thought begins to fade.

Personal Journal

_____

_____

_____

_____ Date _____

DAY 141

Insight

Atoms are mostly space.

Reflections

Meditation clearly illustrates how my thoughts first create themselves and disappear, no different from atomic particles that come into being, only to return to the mystical landscape from which they arise. The thoughts linger a while, and then melt back into immaterial existence. Creativity abounds in the universe.

Meditation

At times, it can be like trying to calm the powerful, unrelenting winds of a hurricane, but soon you will find yourself flowing inward toward spirituality, instead of outward toward the world. Watch everything come and go, calmly, peacefully, and without regret. There is so much more to discover and, when it is discovered, your present perceived reality will be but an abstract dream. Continue with your nose tip concentration.

Personal Journal

_____
_____
_____
_____ *Date* _____

DAY 142

Insight

Images cloud the light of reality.

Reflections

I am becoming increasingly aware of the many mistakes I seem to be making in practice, but perhaps it is impossible to make mistakes. Maybe my practice, as poor as I believe it to be, is affecting me more than I realize. I can't look at the mistakes—those are in the past. The only thing I can look at is my breath, at this very moment, in what is called time.

Meditation

Lighten your diet if possible, maybe some yogurt, a few more vegetables, fruits, and nuts. Don't do anything drastic; the body is made up of only chemicals, and radical changes might produce severe reactions. Experiment for a few months to see which foods improve meditation. Where and when you physically meditate might have an effect as well. Try meditating outdoors at times. Continue with your nose tip concentration.

Personal Journal

_____

_____

_____

_____ Date _____

Mental Bliss

Your practice is deepening. A mental feeling of bliss might now reinforce the wonderful physical happiness that you may have been experiencing. Happiness has a temporary quality of sudden rapture, whereas bliss is more consistent. Bliss has a quality of contentment that is calmer, similar to the feeling one has after achieving a goal—the glowing after-effect of a happy experience. Where happiness has a feeling of fleeting excitement, bliss has a more mature quality of lasting satisfaction.

During concentration, you will experience a brief respite from negative thoughts. It is a long-needed holiday for the mind. Thoughts connected with greed, anger, worry, agitation, and so forth disappear for only a moment, but that is long enough to uncover the happiness and bliss that has remained smothered under these troubling drives and emotions. This bliss increases as practice continues, but be careful of attaching to it, for it will change. The calmness and joy experienced by merging with your concentration object is a taste of the unification that will soon be experienced. If you don't experience happiness or bliss, but are able to remain on your concentration object, don't be concerned. Happiness and bliss, and all experiences for that matter, must give way at some point to insight and wisdom, which is the ultimate goal, so your persistent concentration is what's important. This is what will eventually bring insight and wisdom to fruition.

DAY 143

Insight

Know one thing completely...and know everything.

Reflections

A good mystery holds my attention, but once the mystery is solved, the book is put away. What mysteries can never be solved? Perhaps an insect will never understand Shakespeare, and similarly my mind will never know many things as well, but this is all becoming irrelevant, as questions become increasingly irrelevant. Already, I have seen a part of me that is not dependent upon knowledge.

Meditation

Begin with your preliminary exercises followed by nose tip concentration.

Personal Journal

_____

_____

_____

_____ Date _____

Single-Mindedness

You might find yourself abiding in this beautiful happiness and bliss for some time, even thinking that this is it! I'm enlightened! when suddenly the sobering experience of single-mindedness could arise. Extremely penetrating, this one-pointedness of mind is a gateway into subsequent, deeper states of concentration, and as such, it exudes a unique confidence. This bold confidence, felt as an expansion in your heart, expresses itself as an overwhelming certainty, particularly when noticing common, everyday things. Upon seeing a new leaf, you may suddenly understand, actually know within the depths of your being, that life is never-ending. These five phenomena: applied thought, sustained thought, happiness, bliss, and single-mindedness comprise the first stage of concentration. Whether they are experienced separately, seemingly simultaneously, or not at all, don't be overly concerned about them. They will either occur or not occur, independently of any effort except your attempt to remain concentrated on your object. Quiet, steady meditation accompanied by no experiences whatsoever is as powerful as meditation accompanied by many experiences, considering that the goal of meditation is insight and wisdom, or freedom. So don't be concerned if you have no experiences. Just meditate, and then one day...

DAY 144

Insight

It is extremely dark when the world disappears; pitch black when heaven vanishes.

Reflections

Do I have enough courage to dive into the unknown that lurks beyond my understanding? A great deal of my perceived security depends on my knowledge. This knowledge, however, only goes as far as the images I have created in my mind. Can I remain within that darkness of no understanding where both heaven and Earth are forsaken? How could anyone, other than a true spiritual warrior, have the nerve to look beyond the images that shape his or her life?

Meditation

Continue with your nose tip concentration.

Personal Journal

_____

_____

_____

_____ _Date_ _____

DAY 145

Insight

Palm trees bending in the storm, never breaking.

Reflections

Doubt attacks in many ways: Why should I turn my back on everything important in my life and become a solitary meditator? I could possibly grow apart from my friends. I'm not very good at meditation anyway; I'm not getting anywhere. Maybe I can never change. I should be ashamed, only thinking of myself by embarking on this illogical quest for enlightenment. I'm putting myself in unnecessary danger by experimenting with my mind and I will be defenseless against unexpected things that could happen. I'm not destined to hide in a room, I was born to have a fulfilling life!

This is how my mind creates doubt, and it is exceptionally good at it. But it's too late. I've seen things that I could never have experienced without meditation, I know that there is more than the obvious, and my life is changing in many ways. Warriors never retreat, even in the face of devastating doubt, and I'm becoming a true warrior.

Meditation

Wherever your practice takes you, be satisfied. This quality of gentle persistence, with no purpose, will bring you to your next phase. Here, you will first "strike the bell" by directing your mind to the feeling of the breath in your nose, followed by your concentration becoming steady and sustained where the "bell" sounds continuously with no further directing required. Then feelings of happiness, bliss, and one-pointedness of mind might come over some meditators. If this happens, don't force your mind back to your breath immediately but remain aware of whatever feeling arises for a while and become familiar with it. Don't try to stay with the feeling, but don't try to dismiss it either. It will move along by itself. Continue with your nose tip concentration.

Personal Journal

_____

_____

_____

_____ *Date* _____

DAY 146

Insight

The glitter of the world blinds fools forever.

Reflections

· Things I have been fond of in the past are losing their appeal. I notice some sadness creeping in. I find myself becoming emotional at least once a week, if not more often, with feelings best described as those felt when standing on the tarmac, tearfully waving good-bye to a dear friend you know you will never see again. This is probably a sign that my practice is deepening, and although the pain is melancholy, it is painful nonetheless. I guess I know why I have always attached so tightly to things; it just hurts too much to let them go, but go these attachments must, as all things seem to do in time.

Meditation

Meditation will present you with many uncertainties. Whatever occurs, regard everything equally. Observe it, note it, and then let it go its own way. Good, bad—enlightening or frightening—it matters not. Similar to bad dreams that you know are unreal, frightening things that arise are harmless if they are understood merely as passing occurrences. These scary things do serve a purpose, however, training you to remain steady within your concentration regardless of circumstances. Everything is transient, and when it moves on, you will still be there, for now. Continue with your nose tip concentration.

Personal Journal

_____

_____

_____

_____ *Date* _____

DAY 147

Insight

Rivulets of rain running toward the stream, joyfully returning to their Source.

Reflections

I have the idea that I am here and you are there, while my Source is somewhere else. Is it possible, at some profound level, deeper than my perceived physical and psychological individuality, that there is a singularity? What deep-rooted beliefs and opinions would I have to relinquish to realize this state of oneness?

Meditation

Confidence in your practice is undoubtedly building now, and hints of spirituality should be apparent even though different people experience these hints in different ways. To avoid delays in your next stage, be very careful of symbolizing. Building a grandiose image of yourself as a great meditator will not only make you hard to live with, but will prevent you from experiencing better things later. Continue with your nose tip concentration.

Personal Journal

_____
_____
_____
_____ *Date* _____

DAY 148

Insight

Getting things done, but not doing anything!

Reflections

Taking meditation into daily life is happening involuntarily. To my surprise, I find myself sitting a little straighter by taking better care of my responsibilities and not being so much of a pest. Life situations seem to come and go, no different from the ever-present thoughts that flit by in meditation, and I find myself sometimes observing life no differently than I observe my breath during practice.

Meditation

Steady practice, day in and day out with no anticipation is the key. Calmness must be developed before your mind relaxes into the practice. Continue with your nose tip concentration.

Personal Journal

_____

_____

_____

_____ Date _____

New Object

At some point during meditation, your mind will become confident in its ability to focus, without distraction, on the feeling of your breath, an assurance similar to completely trusting someone to drive you cross country so that you can sit back, relax, and enjoy the scenery. This confidence leads to your next important step in concentration, where after striking the bell (going to the meditation object), and after the bell rings continuously (when you can stay on the ojbect without distraction), the mind may find itself observing itself! This extraordinary occurence can be accompanied by happiness, bliss, and one-pointedness of mind.

This experience can be comprehended in many ways. It might appear as something *light-like* in your mind. Or it could be a feeling of bliss to the tenth power, or a mental emptiness or blank screen; a feeling of the breath itself moving in and out of every pore or through the mind, or luminously flooding the body, and your mind will be mysteriously attracted to it remaining effort-lessly absorbed in it. Initially you will follow old habits and return to your old object. When this happens, this new experience of *mind observing the mind* will temporarily cease. When this back and forth between your old meditation object and the new one ceases, you will have reached a new stage in your practice where you can reside solely in your new ojbect of concentration. At this point, your undivided attention will be effortlessly absorbed into this new object with no further awareness of your posture or breathing.

DAY 149

Insight

The greatest disrespect is worry.

Reflections

Sometimes, I don't worry about a thing. It happens when I'm in love! No fear can penetrate that. What replaced the fear?

Meditation

Continue with your nose tip concentration, or, if a new meditation object happens to appear, concentrate on that and remain intensely concentrated on it. Adjust your posture when you first begin meditating, but then don't concern yourself with it. Don't continually check or adjust it now. It is more important to devote all your attention to this new object, if it in fact appears. Most meditators will not experience this new object, and if you don't, this is not a problem. If it doesn't emerge, don't be concerned or try to imagine one appearing.

Personal Journal

_____

_____

_____

_____ *Date* _____

DAY 150

Insight

Our personal world, no matter how small, becomes our universe.

Reflections

I can't resist the idea of accomplishment. It keeps me so completely occupied and makes me feel alive. But I've noticed disappointment creeping in soon after each goal is accomplished, urging me to immediately set another. Why not be spontaneous instead, no longer involving myself with this goal-setting? Probably because it would be boring—at least that's how I perceive it to be. Without plans and goals, how would I define myself? It's still about me, isn't it?

Meditation

Continue with concentration, either the nose tip or your new meditation object.

Personal Journal

_____

_____

_____

_____ _Date_ _____

DAY 151

Insight

Accumulations are but pesky barnacles on our sailboat.

Reflections

I tend to collect things and then cherish them, not the least being my unique personality that I unfortunately must prop up continuously. I feel so relieved when my thoughts abate during meditation.

Meditation

Try not to analyze your practice; just flow with it. Always begin your sessions with the preliminary exercises and then nose tip concentration, where happiness, bliss, and one-pointedness of mind might arise. At any time, even while remaining immersed in this happiness, bliss, and one-pointedness, your new meditation object could replace your nose tip concentration. When this happens, or when the "mind observes the mind," no longer will there be a strong feeling of somebody meditating, or the idea of a meditation object, or any awareness of posture or breathing. You will merely absorb into this new object. This object will always appear to be very consistent, always looking or feeling the same, and at some point may appear to drop into your heart area. Learn to bring up this meditation object every time you practice, always beginning with your three deep breaths, opening your seven centers, and concentrating on your nose tip. Then just let the mind find this unique object that it has discovered by itself, if it has. Everything will disappear except for this steady focus, bathed in happiness, bliss, and unwavering attention. If the object becomes a white light, expand it to about the size of your head and dwell with it.

Personal Journal 🪷

_____

_____

_____

_____ Date _____

DAY 152

Insight

Courageous are the seekers.

Reflections

It takes courage, this quest for enlightenment. A frightening precipice seems to exist between my illusions and the truth of enlightenment, and I'm deathly afraid of heights! My strong mind feels that it is taking a big risk.

Meditation

Continue with concentration of the nose tip or of your new meditation object. Do whatever is necessary in your life and in your practice to help maintain this state of "mind watching mind" if it arises. The ability to repeat this stage of meditation is extremely important in your practice. It is essential to find your way back easily, not only to this stage, but to areas even more refined that might be developed later on as well. When out in daily life, keep your concentration object in mind at all times. Begin with a few minutes in the morning and work toward keeping it in mind all day. Please keep in mind to be careful when operating machinery or driving while concentrating on this object.

Personal Journal

_____
_____
_____
_____ Date _____

DAY 153

Insight

Steps toward nothingness.

Reflections

Like climbing the steep face of an icy mountain, I must be certain that each foothold is secure before taking the next step. I must know who I am right now, and be who I am, fully, consciously—even if I don't particularly like myself. Only when I know myself completely can I then proceed.

Meditation

Now your practice is deepening. Your six limited senses—what you experience when you see, feel, hear, taste, or touch something, or when your mind thinks—is restricted by space, distance, time, and dimension. These senses become quiescent and dormant when and if your spiritual essence emerges, and it is this underlying consciousness that your mind forms as an image and takes it as a meditation object. This underlying consciousness cannot be understood or explained, but it can be experienced as an image. Remaining with whatever your mind perceives this image to be, and then deepening it, sets the stage for subsequent steps. A word of caution: If you read ahead in this guide or anticipate any of these things, the anticipation itself will distract your mind with thoughts and slow your progress. Additionally, something could develop or happen other than what's being explained, perhaps even more refined. Don't forget, your mind is blind to areas of spirituality, so never allow the mind to take the lead in meditation—and be careful in life as well. The mind must be engaged in order to survive in the world, but only to a point before it becomes counterproductive. Continue with concentration, either nose tip or your new meditation object.

Personal Journal

_____

_____

_____

_____ *Date* _____

DAY 154

Insight

Like hasty, broiling ocean waves finally touching shore, only to recede again, we lap the shores of our desires.

Reflections

In daily life, I'm beginning to notice my physical and mental feelings, just as I notice my thoughts during meditation. I find myself watching my frustration, joy, kindness, and aversion without necessarily buying into them. More often than not now, I can simply watch them come and go.

Meditation

When your concentration object appears, and outer sense experiences vanish, you will disappear as well, perhaps giving you the first real taste of no-self. This experience cannot be accurately interpreted by your mind, but in a strange way, you will remember it as an immense confidence and knowing. Continue with concentration, either nose tip or your new meditation object.

Personal Journal

_____
_____
_____
_____ Date _____

DAY 155

Insight

I dreamed of life. Or is life the dream?

Reflections

My mind goes nonstop, from the moment I awaken until the moment I fall asleep, and even then it continues in dreams. I particularly notice its compulsive activity in the mornings before my days start. I'm finding that if I can watch it here, then a good possibility exists that I can continue to monitor it for the rest of the day.

Meditation

You will eventually see your thoughts as merely computer files based on nothing more than dead storage. Because these thoughts remain in their own world, distant from your spiritual essence, you can allow them to go their own way and do their own thing. When you no longer see thought as important, thought will become abstract and you will no longer see it as yourself. Your fledgling spiritual sense will then increasingly strengthen until it becomes your new, wonderful identity. Continue with concentration, either nose tip or your new meditation object.

Personal Journal

_____

_____

_____

_____ Date _____

A Year to Enlightenment

DAY 156

Insight

Secure in my dreams, dawn comes knocking.

Reflections

What are my refuges? My bank account, my excellent health, my beliefs, my relationships? A refuge is somewhere to hide, and when I hide, I can't see things, and when I refuse to see, there are no further possibilities. Then I'm as good as dead.

Meditation

Your interests and passions were previously tied to the world, but now they draw themselves inwardly, like a magnet, toward your newly discovered spiritual essence. As you move from worldly influences into a true spiritual life, the seven centers you open before each practice now begin to energize and spin. Continue with concentration, either nose tip or your new meditation object.

Personal Journal

_____

_____

_____

_____ *Date* _____

DAY 157

Insight

Find it quickly, find it slowly. But find you it will!

Reflections

It's too late to go back. Stopping now would position me between two opposing desires—worldly and spiritual—a most unwelcome situation. Neither desire would be satisfied. I must keep striving until striving is no longer necessary. I will know.

Meditation

Your new spiritual sensibilities that are developing will create changes in your life, compelling you to alter things that impede your progress. Be ready for transformations. Go slowly. Continue with concentration, either nose tip or your new meditation object, allowing either of them to drop into your heart and remain there if that's what develops.

Personal Journal

_____

_____

_____

_____ Date _____

DAY 158

Insight

The meek will inherit much more than the Earth.

Reflections

When I surrender the supports that I have relied upon for a lifetime, I find myself navigating through turbulent waters. I can't give up both the heaven that I have counted on so desperately, as well as my world, without feeling a crushing loss. This leaves me with no footing. Maybe this spiritual poverty is exactly where I must be to free-fall...down this mountain I have created for myself, the one I have been struggling to climb. If I must, I shall live in complete poverty, both material and spiritual.

Meditation

As your spiritual essence alters your emotions, you will revisit life from entirely different viewpoints. Love will now be less restrictive, like the sun's warmth that covers the entire earth. Small, petty annoyances and attachments will no longer plague you as your greed and hatred begin to calm down. You will reside peacefully, regardless of external circumstances, still maintaining your responsibilities but from a standpoint of detachment—a compassionate detachment. Continue with concentration, either nose tip or your new meditation object.

Personal Journal

_____
_____
_____
_____ *Date* _____

DAY 159

Insight

It is crouched deep inside, waiting for the exact moment!

Reflections

I'm finding it increasingly difficult to push or hurry things along. I want to only sit and wait now, slowly and confidently surrendering to that which is growing in my heart.

Meditation

During this stage in your practice, don't necessarily restrict the time allotted for meditation. Continue concentrating as long as necessary. Your spiritual sensibilities and your spiritual essence are taking charge.

Personal Journal

_____

_____

_____

_____ _Date_ _____

DAY 160

Insight

The moment is eternal.

Reflections

If I could remain focused in this present moment without sneaking a look either back at memories or ahead anticipating plans, what would I discover there?

Meditation

Don't wobble in your practice, but don't take charge either. Passively let the practice move you. You are making good progress, for a beginner! Continue with concentration.

Personal Journal

_____

_____

_____

_____ *Date* _____

DAY 161

Insight

Make your plans today; tomorrow's being will surely pay.

Reflections

Only in this moment can I raise my consciousness beyond worldly considerations, even though worldly considerations must be acknowledged. I have little choice when it comes to maintaining my body and fulfilling my responsibilities, but surprisingly, life in the world is becoming easier with this new awareness. It is becoming efficient and full of love, and I'm finding myself to be neither a doormat, nor a tyrant. It is only when my mind takes root again in my self and begins doing the planning, that untold difficulties arise.

Meditation

Always begin with your exercises and nose tip concentration until your new object arises. If there is no new object, this is fine. Never force a new object to arise, just carry on with your practice. If one does arise, hold your new object close, even when not meditating, keeping it in mind when you first awaken, and when you are falling asleep– –always. Meditation is not separate from life; it becomes life, just as life becomes a meditation.

Personal Journal

_____

_____

_____

_____ Date _____

A Year to Enlightenment

DAY 162

Insight

Why is a snowflake so amazing to a child? Maybe because nobody told her what to expect.

Reflections

Is disappointment in life connected to expectation? I dream about how it should be, and when it isn't, my sense of fairness seems, in some strange way, violated. What would it be like to have no expectations? Dull? Perhaps boring? Maybe I enjoy my rollercoaster ride of ups and downs, subconsciously causing them myself just for the excitement. What happens when the excitement stops? How do I feel then? How do I react?

Meditation

Continue with your regular practice. If your special meditation object doesn't appear, see what does appear and watch that. The feeling of the breath is always a refuge to return to if necessary. Be careful of thoughts—they can be subtle.

Personal Journal

_____
_____
_____
_____ Date _____

DAY 163

Insight

Do great things, but only with duty in mind.

Reflections

What kind of personality do I have: faithful, greedy, intelligent, hateful, deluded, speculative? It could even be a combination, but I know that one or two inclinations prevail. Humankind seems to have developed a personality as well, one of greed, hatred, and confusion in its efforts to survive. These are sensual cravings, wanting things to go our way, wanting things to happen, wanting things not to happen. Our worldly activities are so enmeshed with scheming, competition, and ambition—greedy for money, competing for land, and killing each other over these things as if they would somehow free us from servitude. The world, which we comprise, has become completely economic, leaving love and understanding at the altar. Where has this taken us? Where will it lead? Is there any hope of it ever changing? Is there any hope of me ever changing?

Meditation

By ignoring thoughts in meditation, you temporarily step out of your personality, simply because your personality is created by thoughts. Mind, however, is matter, and is always being influenced by spirit. Therefore, your base tendencies will change to the extent that your spiritual essence emerges. Continue with concentration.

Personal Journal

_____
_____
_____
_____ Date _____

A Year to Enlightenment

DAY 164

Insight

Seclusion...how precious!

Reflections

I sat on the beach yesterday. Groups of birds busily looked toward the ocean for their tidbits to arrive, while I searched for my sustenance as well. It was peaceful out there, with the alternating whooshing and silence of the waves, the relentless sun. Then, suddenly, I let everything go for a moment. I was just there, on the beach with the waves. How easy that was.

Meditation

The greed, hatred, and confusion plaguing you for so long now surrenders during meditation. It's so liberating! Continue with concentration, either nose tip or your new meditation object.

Personal Journal

_____
_____
_____
_____ Date _____

DAY 165

Insight

The candle burns at both ends.

Reflections

Meditation is definitely affecting my life. This new life, in turn, is deepening my meditation. From this moment on, I am determined to explore humankind's distress and discover how to end it in myself, by speaking with a kind voice, acting responsibly in every way, and earning a living that causes no harm. I will be steadfast in my practice as well, being ever mindful, inquiring into truth, and concentrating my mind.

Meditation

Perhaps you are now experiencing some lucidity. This clarity will increase when you are able to see with new eyes. The transparency will increase slowly, however, so that you are able to absorb the changes occurring. Stay true to your practice, every day and every moment. What else is there to do? Continue with concentration, either nose tip or your new meditation object.

Personal Journal

_____

_____

_____

_____ _Date_ _____

A Year to Enlightenment

DAY 166

Insight

Question everything.

Reflections

I feel that my psychological life is on the line. A sense of danger prevails. Without danger, practice doesn't seem to deepen. This inward journey would not have been possible within the context of the life I was living, a life of ease and decadence. My mind constantly flowed out toward the world of sensual desires, thirsting for excitement and caught up in hardened opinions and a basic ignorance of reality. Only critical situations and danger had the power to still my wild mind, and this I intuitively understood from the beginning. This left me no alternative but to turn my back on the familiar world I knew and seek places within where my restless mind might calm down enough for me to see with new eyes. Once these new eyes began to open, there was no going back.

Meditation

Stay concentrated, never wavering. This is a crucial period in your spiritual development.

Personal Journal

_____

_____

_____

_____ Date _____

DAY 167

Insight

You come apart at the end.

Reflections

When that crushing blow comes, I'd better be ready. Soldiers would be lost in battle without training, and I will be lost as well, unless I am intimately acquainted with my spiritual essence. I must practice with resolve, while I can.

Meditation

Steady. Steady. Let your practice point the way, as you fall into deeper states. Continue with concentration, either nose tip or your new meditation object.

Personal Journal

_____
_____
_____
_____ *Date* _____

Stage 2:
Applied and Sustained
Attention Abandoned

The feeling of *striking the bell* and the *bell sounding continuously* now disappears! Only your concentration object, surrounded by happiness, bliss, confidence, and single-mindedness will remain. Wisdom, being discriminating and extremely mindful, clearly perceives that applied and sustained attention is susceptible to thought, and therefore is undesirable. Single-mindedness will be the quality that wants to prevail at this point, but happiness and bliss restrict it.

At this stage, stop monitoring your posture or the lengths of your breaths. Once you establish your posture, pay no further attention to anything except remaining completely at one with your meditation object. Your meditation object might change now as well, into a feeling of single-mindedness or a feeling of silence that somehow drops into your heart. If it changes into something, whatever that may be, just allow it to happen. There is only *knowing* now, as the mind rests. Don't be concerned about extending the out breath, and don't worry if the breath seems to stop.

Once the mind becomes calm, don't disturb it. Let it remain calm for as long as it wishes, or until you feel fatigued. Don't worry about any responsibilities now; this is too important to disrupt. Use mindfulness at this point to maintain this calm state of mind. If something causes the mind to abruptly come out of this calm, it will be difficult to get the calm back next time because the mind will lose some confidence. So, come out of your calm slowly and peacefully. It is very important to remember how you were able to attain this calm, because this is how you will return to it.

DAY 168

Insight

A true warrior knows his enemy, thoroughly.

Reflections

I'm beginning to notice my arrogance. I see it in my strong opinions, views which are usually based on nothing more than what I've read or heard. I hold tight to these opinions because it's easier than inquiring deeper—that would take energy, and could prove me wrong. Opinions become my security, and whether they are true or not is unimportant. My adversary is simply wrong. Why should I look into his motives? It is easier to defeat him than to understand him. Arrogance is so shallow and distasteful, just seeing it in myself is disgusting, and I can only hope that I change quickly. Perhaps the seeing, in itself, will help me get beyond all this.

Meditation

Continue with concentration.

Personal Journal

_____

_____

_____

_____ Date _____

Stage 3: Happiness Abandoned

After your preliminary exercises, begin each session by directing your mind to your breath, striking the bell, and sustaining the tone (applying attention to your meditation object and then sustaining that attention). This might be followed by stages of happiness and possibly other occurrences, including the arising of a spiritual meditation object, which will replace the feeling of the nose tip as your focus. Now, however, something changes. As happiness arises, you become acutely aware of happiness's frenzied activity. This momentary insight, which is a new awareness, allows you to escape the disturbance of happiness! Now, with only bliss and equanimity remaining, your practice really takes a turn toward stillness. Here, you dwell only in equanimity, bliss, and mindfulness, watching everything without partiality. You will be neither happy nor depressed, neither striving nor slack, and although bliss is still experienced, you will no longer feel necessarily attached to it. This stage is very mature.

Occasionally, you will sit like a stone statue during meditation, with no possibility of being aroused. The body feels no pain or pleasure. You will not be able to hear or see, and therefore you should program your mind beforehand for when you want to rouse yourself from this state. Because of its suspended animation aspect, you can remain seated and unmoving for hours at a time. Some have remained unmoving for days.

DAY 169

Insight

Pity those who stumble blindly through life, attempting to dramatize the mundane.

Reflections

Are the depths of meditation affecting me? Something is going on far beyond the reaches of my mind. And because my mind is the limit of my intelligence, where does that leave me?

Meditation

Continue with concentration.

Personal Journal

_____
_____
_____
_____ *Date* _____

DAY 170

Insight

Pull gently on tangled fishing line.

Reflections

I have a tendency to attack my practice aggressively, forcing things in little ways, but I'm learning that these attacks always lead to retreats. Things will come to me without effort someday, when the time is right, and then I won't be required to chase after them.

Meditation

With these new qualities of equanimity and bliss influencing your practice, you will acquire tremendous courage. No longer fearful, you will soon openly acknowledge that your perceived past security and happiness were mere fictions, impermanent, void of any substantial reality, and the cause of incalculable pain. Everything will be seen as having been a terrible misunderstanding of transient occurrences, causing untold suffering by leading you to believe that the occurrences were somehow substantial. This kind of sober insight and realization prohibits the return of happiness in your practice, and keeps you within the realm of equanimity. Continue with concentration.

Personal Journal 🪷

_____

_____

_____

_____ Date _____

DAY 171

Insight

A time to dream. A time to love. A time to die. What an amazing illusion time is!

Reflections

I am beginning to see that time is a trick of my consciousness. Doesn't everything occur in only this one moment, making each moment eternal? How can one moment, so small and fleeting, expand into eternity? How can something the size of a pea, as astrophysicists claim, expand into a universe?

Meditation

The return of happiness in meditation (and a return to your fictional security in life) remains a constant threat. Your spiritual essence, however, will soon deepen your practice and dispel any possibility of happiness's return. Total mindfulness watches over your practice at this time, along with bliss, equanimity, and full awareness. Continue with concentration.

Personal Journal

_____

_____

_____

_____ *Date* _____

DAY 172

Insight

Whatever you carry is surplus; throw it overboard!

Reflections

I'm trying to travel unencumbered, but what is it that I am still hanging on to?

Meditation

Your meditation becomes motionless, wrapped in bliss, mindfulness, and awareness. Similar to a child gazing into a starry night lost in wonderment, its vastness overwhelms you. Continue with concentration.

Personal Journal

_____

_____

_____

_____ *Date* _____

DAY 173

Insight

All that you meet—let it depart happy.

Reflections

I am seeing new, strange things that aren't necessarily connected with this gross body of mine. But here I am! My body must breathe...and my spirit understands.

Meditation

You are approaching your next level of concentration. Here, your spirit will lead you. Don't allow your mind to interfere. Mind is stealthy and always remains a surreptitious, intervening threat, so watch everything with increased interest but don't allow yourself to become caught up in it. This is a tricky balancing act that only comes with practice. Continue with concentration.

Personal Journal

_____

_____

_____

_____ Date _____

DAY 174

Insight

The impatient forsake it. But it will wait for them, too.

Reflections

I am becoming less concerned with my progress. Concern and progress seem to be connected to my mind, while my spiritual essence never seems to be concerned about anything. With what would it be concerned?

Meditation

Is a suspicion arising regarding this bliss that dominates your practice? With your developing awareness, monitor this bliss carefully. Continue with concentration.

Personal Journal

_____

_____

_____

_____ _Date_ _____

DAY 175

Insight

It is in the heavens. It is everywhere around us. It is us!

Reflections

How would I begin to fully describe my experience of this spiritual essence? Formless, timeless, beyond space? Is it beyond nothingness, beyond consciousness, beyond perception, beyond anything I can think of? It expresses itself in the myriad of forms, including me, and because there is no possibility of its destruction, a part of me cannot be destroyed either. Still, a stubborn perception remains—that I am separate and isolated from this unborn, undying, and uncreated Source.

Meditation

This bliss will flood your body and mind, lingering for some time even after meditation. Mindfulness and equanimity will linger as well, and the combination of these three will create a powerful, compassionate, and affectionate indifference that will seep into every pore of your life, at levels never before experienced. Continue with concentration.

Personal Journal

_____

_____

_____

_____ _Date_ _____

A Year to Enlightenment

DAY 176

Insight

At times, it's unresponsive to our petty desires, but never to our true longing.

Reflections

Experiencing that spiritual essence within moves my entire being. Studying books, accepting beliefs, or listening to teachers will never instill that passion. I touch it when I silence my mind and face my emptiness, and only then do the past ideas, teachings, misconceptions, and indoctrinations fade from memory, leaving only a pure, bright, calm mind. Only then does my core, my absolute reality, surface from within my own consciousness, enabling me to make the surprising discovery that this fundamental nature is not merely in me, it is all of me.

Meditation

While you are immersed in this bliss and equanimity, any physical pain ceases as your spiritual essence suspends normal sensations by influencing matter itself. Continue with concentration.

Personal Journal

_____
_____
_____
_____ Date _____

DAY 177

Insight

Worldly pleasures—like catching a snake by its tail.

Reflections

The worldly things I depend upon become my blackmailers. I always pay in one way or another.

Meditation

Let's review your steps: Begin with the preliminary three breaths and then cycle through your seven centers. This balances mind and body and reduces any tendencies to go off track. If your mind-watching-mind object is present the moment you sit down, or before you sit down to meditate, perform the preliminary exercises before concentrating on it. If it doesn't arise, proceed with nose tip concentration. Any brief happiness that appears will now be quickly abandoned as your sensitive mind identifies the danger of happiness, and only your object of concentration, bathed in bliss and equanimity, will remain. Continue your concentration.

Personal Journal

_____
_____
_____
_____ Date _____

DAY 178

Insight

You will never progress...but there is progress.

Reflections

What is it that will liberate me? Is it spiritual enlightenment itself, or is it my attempt to achieve enlightenment? Since my efforts are admittedly feeble, it must be enlightenment, itself. I can only wait patiently.

Meditation

Never become an experienced meditator, always remain a beginner. Work on this seriously, particularly if your personality leans toward the intellectual or speculative side. Approach each moment with new eyes. Continue with concentration.

Personal Journal

_____
_____
_____
_____ *Date* _____

DAY 179

Insight

With motionless mind, I watch the forest in its solitude.

Reflections

The woods are cool in the mornings, the pines barely moving in the whispers of early light. At times, I wish I could live out here, alone, but how could I ever be alone? Look what surrounds me. The beauty of this patient stillness brings me to the brink of tears.

Meditation

Continue to observe bliss suspiciously, out of the corner of your eye. Continue with concentration.

Personal Journal

_____

_____

_____

_____ Date _____

DAY 180

Insight

Everything the same, each in its peculiar way.

Reflections

Maybe I'll leave this busy world, for just a few years, and actually live alone in those woods. What would I discover about myself out there?

Meditation

Start every practice with no expectations, as if it was your first session. Planning to begin with the breath and then quickly attain higher states will stop your progress in its tracks, so be certain that you allow your spiritual essence to lead. Always begin with your exercises, followed by your nose tip concentration as usual unless your spiritual object is present. If it is, then go to it. What happens after that depends on something else, not you. Authentic meditation experiences never come from personal will. They deepen by themselves. Observing the feeling of your breath is crucial, but attempting to create deep states of meditation with your mind is as fruitless as a weevil trying to burrow into granite mountains.

Personal Journal

_____
_____
_____
_____ *Date* _____

DAY 181

Insight

A shot rings out. A deer falls. The universe is diminished.

Reflections

When I seek power or fame, doesn't that expose an apparent weakness in myself? When I stop seeking completely, yet maintain a bright mind, what does that reveal?

Meditation

Continue with concentration.

Personal Journal

_____
_____
_____
_____ Date _____

Stage 4:
Bliss Abandoned

As your practice develops, suspicions deepen about the bliss you are experiencing, until one day you finally see its potential danger—it is too uncomfortably close to pleasure and pain. Following this insight, bliss immediately disappears! You would think that this wonderful bliss would be sorely missed, because it is closely associated with joy, but surprisingly, it isn't missed at all, because what replaces it is incredibly more mature and satisfying. When you relinquish this joyful bliss that you have been bathing in for so long, what's left? What remains is the unbelievable calmness, composure, and compassionate indifference of equanimity, along with an effortless one-pointed mindfulness of your spiritual object. These are the precursors of deepening meditation. Soon, your mind will experience even more subtle objects of concentration brought about by your spiritual essence, but in the meantime, enjoy this pure equanimity with its spotless mindfulness. At times now, it might seem as if your breathing has stopped. Don't be concerned about this and continue with your practice. If you can overcome your fear of death when the breathing seems to stop, you may have a great insight into the nature of death.

DAY 182

Insight

Do you really seek freedom?

Reflections

With this departure of bliss comes an understanding—that my goal of freedom involves total freedom, not merely freedom from the undesirable, but from the desirable as well. How can ultimate freedom choose between the two? They are co-dependent illusions.

Meditation

Your greed and hatred diminish appreciably now, replaced by equanimity. Equanimity is a tremendous breath of fresh air that supersedes feelings of both pleasure and pain, and is difficult to comprehend without direct experience. Equanimity, however, is not merely the absence of pleasure and pain; it is a different feeling altogether, directly opposed to, but at the same time in harmony with, both of them. Equanimity is evenhanded and unbiased with no agenda, overwhelming even the powerful emotion of bliss. Continue with concentration.

Personal Journal

_____
_____
_____
_____ *Date* _____

DAY 183

Insight

Darkness defines light.

Reflections

Here, at this very moment, within me is everything. How could it be otherwise? All that is required of me is to look! The night sky appears dark, but it's full of light, only lacking something for that light to strike. Am I also not full of light, needing only something that I can illuminate as well?

Meditation

Equanimity has an innate quality that refines mindfulness in an amazing way. With neutral feelings toward everything, your mind sees with different eyes. It has the courage to face reality, a daring that was absent while your mind remained attached and clinging. Your world is still there to enjoy, but now through new lenses. Don't try to analyze this equanimity within the limits of your mind—you can only experience it. Continue with concentration.

Personal Journal

_____

_____

_____

_____ *Date* _____

DAY 184

Insight

Has anything ever really ended? Or begun?

Reflections

If time stretches from here to there, where is here and where is there? Both here and there each have their one moment in time. What if I remained in that one moment...here, and didn't go...there? Would time be any different? Perhaps there is no time. Perhaps it is created by my ideas of it.

Meditation

What could be deeper than this state of equanimity? Surely, you must be thinking that this equanimity is the pinnacle of practice. Actually, you are just beginning! You will always be just beginning. Continue with concentration.

Personal Journal

_____

_____

_____

_____ Date _____

DAY 185

Insight

Fools live to die. Wise ones die to live.

Reflections

What a remarkable thing a tree is, how perfect. What is it that can hold a tiny acorn in its loving hands for one moment before transforming it into a mighty oak of such enormous beauty? Is this a microcosm of the universe, beginning with a seed, then spreading throughout space while dropping its countless kernels? I ponder the brown leaves on the ground. I look at the new, budding leaves in the branches—and I intuitively understand. I understand the renewal of all things. How could I ever die? Many things I will never know, but for today that's not important. In this precious moment, in my heart, everything is flawless. All is perfect...just as it is.

Meditation

The mystical things happening in meditation are coming from within yourself, nowhere else. They have always been there from your very first day of practice. You have always been enlightened, but now you are just beginning to realize it. Meditation, however, is not the only means for these occurrences to arise. These mystical things are not the sole province of meditation practice; they can appear spontaneously to anybody, at any time, leaving him or her somewhat breathless and in awe, and perhaps thinking that they have experienced enlightenment. But they haven't, not yet. To deepen these experiences and really know enlightenment intimately, guidance is required. Your spiritual essence is not far away, just in your heart, but in order for it to surface, it requires a persistent removal of the busy-ness of yourself, one moment at a time. Continue with concentration.

Personal Journal

_____

_____

_____

_____ Date _____

DAY 186

Insight

Trying involves conflict.

Reflections

I can't change myself directly. This would be too aggressive. It would be like trying to kill something. But what am I to do if I can't try to change myself? Remain miserable? No. What I'll do is confront my problem indirectly. I'll go around by the back door and attack in a way that will destroy the root of whatever it is about myself I'm dissatisfied with. I'll finish it off forever instead of just toying with its symptoms. I'll do this by observing what I am, deeply, sincerely, and stopping there. I think that only within this honest observation, without taking action, lies the enormous potentiality of my transformation.

Meditation

With each deepening stage of meditation, your mind, influenced by awareness, will see the previous stage and its flaws. This seeing is what prompts the next stage of development. Never try to create the next stage, only study the present one. In this scrutiny, your attachment to the present stage diminishes, allowing a deeper stage to fill the void. Continue with concentration.

Personal Journal

_____

_____

_____

_____ Date _____

DAY 187

Insight

Sinners in churches, saints in the streets.

Reflections

The problem with violently forcing myself to change is that although I might think I have changed, I haven't. My latent problems remain hidden within. I deceive myself, pretending, for example, that I'm peaceful, maybe going as far as exhibiting some kind of profound exterior, but never changing fundamentally. I merely become a good actor, changing superficially and convincing myself that I'm now a saint.

Meditation

Many things can occur during meditation. It is quite common to have visions, see vivid fields of color, develop powers, or hear voices. Continue your journey despite these distractions, only stopping to notice them for a moment, as you would take in the sights when traveling. Don't become involved with these things—particularly powers that might develop, for they will only delay your progress toward enlightenment. Carry on with concentration.

Personal Journal

_____

_____

_____

_____ Date _____

DAY 188

Insight

Vision requires daring.

Reflections

The way to change myself is to see what I am—and more importantly, to genuinely accept it. This can only be done by not taking direct action. Actions mask my failings, and my failings must remain visible. Not taking action is, on one hand, a very passive thing to do, but on the other, very courageous, and effective. Although I feel as though I am doing nothing, this mere seeing has tremendous power because of its undisturbed (by taking no action) focus.

Meditation

Don't become alarmed if you are absent-minded during daily activities. Your mind has a lot on its plate now and might not take the same interest in worldly affairs that it has in the past. But things will get done. As long as you are practicing correctly, let any unusual occurrences sort themselves out. Don't become too involved with any great schemes hatched by the mind, for example, writing books, traveling to India, or any activity that will disrupt your practice. The deeper you go, the cleverer the mind will become at deflecting your efforts. By now, you should be aware of when you are lost in thought. Continue with concentration.

Personal Journal

_____

_____

_____

_____ _Date_ _____

DAY 189

Insight

Deception fears its enemy—observation.

Reflections

When I intensely observe a problem for long periods, without bias or without any attempt to solve it, it seems to volunteer a solution all by itself. No matter what I do in life, whether it is living in my comfortable home, or living in a cave, I am always observing. And what is it that I observe? It is the truth or falsity of every situation. Why do I tirelessly sort things out and try to comprehend the truth? It is because I resent being misled. I despise being deceived or disappointed.

Meditation

As you continue to watch this unique equanimity, there will be hints that it is somewhat suspect. This insight will seem incredulous, but true. Don't concern yourself with this now; it is just a deepening of practice. If your practice progresses as it should, your mind will never have anything to hang on to for long. Continue with concentration.

Personal Journal

_____

_____

_____

_____ *Date* _____

DAY 190

Insight

Self: the ultimate dependency.

Reflections

Can I begin to observe this truth I so desperately seek by facing what it is that I am dependent upon? Perhaps I rely on the people I cherish, or a cause that I believe in, something I would miss terribly if I lost it. The question is, is it possible to be free, completely free of this dependency no matter how important it seems to be? Isn't dependency always connected to the past, with images and illusions that are not truth? Perhaps only when my dependencies are finally resolved will I come upon the threshold of total freedom. Perhaps dependency begins right here at home, with this enormous self that I have created, and with which I am so attached.

Meditation

Your experiences so far—the striking of the bell, remaining with the tone of the bell, happiness, bliss, one-pointedness of mind, equanimity, and mindfulness—all have a dangerous quality: their close proximity to the material world. As your refined mind notices this, there will be an instant longing to escape their influence. Continue with concentration.

Personal Journal

_____

_____

_____

_____ Date _____

A Year to Enlightenment

DAY 191

Insight

Truth guards those who practice.

Reflections

Can I become attached and dependent upon truth? I suppose I could, but perhaps I am dependent upon only the concept of truth. How could I become attached to the actuality of truth? It moves far too fast for attachments to form. Truth always seems to be only in this one, alive, and unpredictable moment, but my unrefined consciousness isn't. Much work remains to establish an insightful mind strong enough to pierce through my many and varied deceptions. Until I can walk through the forest and look at a leaf as if I am seeing a leaf for the first time in my life, and then see the next leaf as the first leaf I have ever seen, I will never be able to claim success. What greater gift could there be?

Meditation

This longing to escape the material world might brew for quite a while, until one day your object of concentration, that special object provided by your spiritual essence, will be seen in a very different light. Continue with concentration.

Personal Journal

_____

_____

_____

_____ *Date* _____

Stage 5:
Boundless Space

Begin with your warm-up exercises and nose tip concentration. Happiness, bliss, one-pointedness of mind, equanimity, and your new object of concentration might follow this. Then you abide there. All of this activity, however, will eventually appear to be a bit frantic. Shortly after this acknowledgment of turbulence, your practice will deepen as you notice a very unusual thing: Your meditation object has disappeared! All that remains is the space behind it! As you become increasingly aware that your meditation object is gone, the space will loom ever more ominously. Then, you will become completely immersed in it.

DAY 192

Insight

In a blind world, a one-eyed man is king.

Reflections

I understand many things about meditation, but do I feel them? Until they take root in my heart, my destiny remains unchanged.

Meditation

Begin your practice as usual, with your three breaths and opening your seven centers. Now your meditation object has become boundless space, and neither your breath, the new object given to you by your spiritual essence, nor anything else, is revisited.

Personal Journal

_____

_____

_____

_____ $\mathcal{D}_{ate}$ _____

DAY 193

Insight

One person meditating affects everybody in the world.

Reflections

At this stage in my practice, I find myself sitting alone, self-indulged in meditation. What help can I offer anybody? What help will I be able to offer when and if I'm ever enlightened? Does the presence of an enlightened being, even without direct contact, affect humankind with a kind of psychic osmosis? Could my piddling progress already silently influence others in a positive way?

Meditation

Now direct your mind to this boundless space as you once directed your mind to the feeling of the breath in your nose by striking the bell, as everything else dissolves. Even discernment of matter is overcome in this immaterial state of boundless space.

Personal Journal

_____

_____

_____

_____ Date _____

A Year to Enlightenment

DAY 194

Insight

Direct experience leaves knowledge in its wake.

Reflections

I meditated. I touched my spiritual essence. What would it be like to be immersed in it?

Meditation

Because matter is no longer applicable in this immaterial stage, sensual desires begin to fade. Eternal personality belief and reliance on ceremonies or dogma are now abandoned as well, along with any lingering doubts that meditation practice will lead to freedom. Passage to higher stages of the next world will be assured with the falling away of these three elements: belief in an eternal personality, reliance on religious dogma, and doubt. Continue concentrating on boundless space.

Personal Journal

_____
_____
_____
_____ _Date_ _____

DAY 195

Insight

Increase, leveling, dissolution: the destiny of matter in all the worlds.

Reflections

Meditation deepens when my life is at stake. I have experienced this, for now in meditation, my life, as I know it, is.

Meditation

Your every sense is subdued while in this immaterial state of boundless space. Matter itself is suspended while bodily functions are slowed to a catatonic state. Continue concentrating on boundless space.

Personal Journal

_____

_____

_____

_____ *Date* _____

DAY 196

Insight

The morning mist clears slowly, waiting patiently for the sun's heat.

Reflections

Sometimes when I practice, I experience long, dry periods with seemingly little results. At other times, there is an inkling of meditation's immensity. That's when I'm instilled with an unbelievably strong passion to go on no matter what the cost. It is difficult to explain the feeling, except that I now...know. What I know, I don't know, but I'm certain of something, even though it is still beyond my conceptual abilities.

Meditation

Continue to dwell in infinite space. Your mind will have full knowledge that you're there.

Personal Journal

_____
_____
_____
_____ *Date* _____

DAY 197

Insight

A great warrior you must become.

Reflections

I see three great weapons that must be mastered if I have any hope of freedom. Only when my Sword of Concentration is razor sharp can I move on to mindfulness, where I'll be trained to use that sharp sword to cut through. Then, by using the resulting insight from this mindfulness after cutting through, I will acquire the wisdom necessary to locate the "I" thought, hidden deep inside myself where it will be slain.

Meditation

This endless space is now your base of operations. Give undivided attention to this new home, for it is your sanctuary now.

Personal Journal

_____

_____

_____

_____ Date _____

DAY 198

Insight

Enlightened beings, always masquerading as ordinary people.

Reflections

My mind is a servant to circumstances, a reactionary vehicle and nothing more. Because my mind can be predisposed to react either peacefully or violently depending on the circumstances, where does ultimate truth lie? At what point does my mind no longer react from external conditions? Perhaps only when it concentrates on itself, then thoroughly investigates itself, and finally experiences the resulting insight. Only then will my mind open a crack so that my spiritual essence can change it forever.

Meditation

This boundless space is very peaceful, very beautiful, but there is again something suspicious here. What is it about this space that is suspect? Upon what is it dependent? Continue with boundless space concentration.

Personal Journal

_____

_____

_____

_____ Date _____

DAY 199

Insight

Realization ends searching. Stop. See...you are free!

Reflections

What happens when spokes are removed from a wheel? The wheel collapses, of course. If I remove my spokes, what choice do I have but to fly?

Meditation

Your body is material. Your mind is fine material. Boundless space, however, is the beginning of immaterial states. After you have experienced these three states during concentration, are you finished? No. Then you must use your razor-sharp, concentrated mind to investigate closely in a unique way. For now, however, you still have three additional immaterial states to experience. Continue with boundless space concentration.

Personal Journal

_____

_____

_____

_____ *Date* _____

DAY 200

Insight

Is the significance in arriving, or in what road is taken...or neither?

Reflections

Would my meditation improve faster if I could only find that special place, maybe overseas, where conditions would be supportive for meditators and the people might better understand our plight? But I'm wary of traveling farther than a few feet from my meditation cushion because my mind so loves to take trips—it would rather do anything but face emptiness. Maybe I should take a trip into emptiness!

Meditation

Concentrate on boundless space as if you will remain in it for eternity. This is the only way you will be able to progress. What comes next only arises after your concentration on infinite space is flawless.

Personal Journal

_____

_____

_____

_____ *Date* _____

Stage 6:
Infinite Consciousness

You will be concentrating on boundless space...boundless space...when suddenly your mind will amazingly understand that both your concentration and your perception of space are dependent on consciousness! Immediately, your mind will then begin searching for that which is non-dependent, something that is not the result of a cause. As soon as your mind grasps the fact that this boundless space does depend on consciousness, it will drop space as its meditation object...and embrace infinite consciousness! This will now be your mind's base of concentration as it dwells in this amazing realm of infinite consciousness.

DAY 201

Insight

Truth recognizes fools quickly, and hides itself well from them.

Reflections

I am breaking new ground every moment. Today, I realized that love is an endless land, beginning with selfish love, with which I love one but hate another, and then progressing into love with no limits.

Meditation

Infinite consciousness should dominate your concentration now.

Personal Journal

_____

_____

_____

_____ _Date_ _____

DAY 202

Insight

Teachers everywhere.

Reflections

Wherever I find myself is where I learn. The more horrible the situation, the more I find out about myself. Just as water seeks its own level, my situations eventually become neutral as well, but it takes time.

Meditation

Continue concentrating on infinite consciousness.

Personal Journal

_____

_____

_____

_____ *Date* _____

A Year to Enlightenment

DAY 203

Insight

Journeys always end. Don't they?

Reflections

What's my hurry? I seem to be foolishly speeding from one stoplight to another. The progress I have made already has altered my destiny, so if I'm still in a hurry to complete my journey, what's my real agenda after the journey is over?

Meditation

Your practice always begins with three deep breaths and opening your seven centers. Then turn your attention to infinite consciousness. Your previous concentration object, boundless space, is now replaced by this consciousness— the consciousness that had previously supported that boundless space.

Personal Journal

_____

_____

_____

_____ $\mathcal{D}_{ate}$ _____

DAY 204

Insight

Children are afraid of the dark, adults of the light.

Reflections

The truth can be intimidating. Secure in my illusions, why would I want to destroy them? It is because my illusions trick me, and I must know exactly where those tricks are. I have noticed that in meditation, my mind is the only trick.

Meditation

Consciousness is immaterial. Mind is fine material. Therefore, consciousness is perceived from an unusual perspective by the mind, for it is observing something foreign to it. Even though this perception can be experienced, it can never be explained. Continue to concentrate on infinite consciousness.

Personal Journal

_____
_____
_____
_____ Date _____

DAY 205

Insight

Journey in darkness with faith fortified by insight.

Reflections

I'm surprised that my mind can be empty while at the same time bright. But this emptiness is not the emptiness I'm familiar with. It is full of life at another level.

Meditation

Even though this infinite consciousness reaches beyond anything you have ever imagined, there is, again, something suspect here. Continue to concentrate on infinite consciousness.

Personal Journal

_____
_____
_____
_____ *Date* _____

DAY 206

Insight

Knowing nothing, watching everything…inside and out.

Reflections

I feel lost. I'm losing touch. But the part I'm losing touch with is the part that can't be trusted.

Meditation

It is possible to develop supernormal powers at this stage. Visions and colors that had previously been amusing might now escalate into the ability to read minds and see into the future. Extremely sensitive hearing could also develop, along with the ability to appear and vanish, fly, or walk on water, or through walls. Be cautious however; cultivating these powers will distract you to the point where enlightenment becomes secondary. It is best to continue with concentration and disregard any powers that arise until you are experienced enough to handle them. Then, of course, why would you need them? Continue to concentrate on infinite consciousness.

Personal Journal 🪷

_____

_____

_____

_____ *Date* _____

DAY 207

Insight

Know what you don't know. Leave it at that.

Reflections

For me to know something for certain, it has to be unchanging. If it moves around, then I can no longer know it, but if it's fixed, of course, then it's dead. Knowing the moment, however, is ineffable, impossible to explain, because the moment is fleeting, and my knowing must be fleeting as well, because both the moment's truth and my knowing are constantly in motion. What could I possibly know that hasn't already changed? I can only be.

Meditation

Having dwelled in infinite consciousness for some time, your mind might begin to notice that this consciousness is troublingly close to your previous base of boundless space, both being dependent upon something and therefore not completely peaceful. Continue to concentrate on infinite consciousness.

Personal Journal

_____
_____
_____
_____ *Date* _____

DAY 208

Insight

The search for answers is folly. Search for questions, then let them ripen.

Reflections

Answers are agonizingly slow for me now, far behind the curve of immediacy. Meditation is teaching me about many things.

Meditation

Your mind might see itself developing an attachment to this infinite consciousness and will perceive this as a danger. At this point, it will begin searching for something even more peaceful and not subject to dependency of any kind. In the mean time, continue to concentrate on infinite consciousness.

Personal Journal

_____
_____
_____
_____ Date _____

DAY 209

Insight

Wisdom is a fiery lake. Swim underwater.

Reflections

Wisdom and insight are arriving in bits and pieces during practice. How can I not resist being caught up in their phenomenal revelations? My determination must be strong to not dwell on these things at this point and keep my distractions to a minimum. Letting go of various insights doesn't mean that I lose them, however, for once aroused, I don't think they can ever be lost. I'm sure these insights will be there for me when needed. In this amazing spiritual life, everything seems to be there precisely when I need it, but not before, and I must genuinely need it, yet never count on it.

Meditation

Where you, the meditator, are now positioned is unintelligible to your common mind. You can only experience it, with the experience itself altering your destiny. This is humankind's potential, merging with something, an essence, that never had a beginning and never ends—humankind's roots. Continue to concentrate on infinite consciousness.

Personal Journal

_____

_____

_____

_____ Date _____

DAY 210

Insight

Spiritual solitude is selfless.

Reflections

How could I, one person, make an impact on the world? Why should I even worry about influencing it—it's doing the best it can under the circumstances, and if it could do better it would. I wonder how many people would be required to change things. Is the power of meditation infectious, so that everybody around me might be influenced without even knowing that I meditate? If I can change myself, surely the world can change as well, because the world is merely a society of me's. I would love to change the world, but only changing me is challenging enough for now.

Meditation

Your experience of daily life will now be altered. It will be quite difficult to continue a normal life without tremendous effort, because your heart has been moved. Similar lifestyle changes are experienced by those who have had near-death or out-of-body experiences, so that everything has changed for them. Everything now changes for you as well. Continue to concentrate on infinite consciousness.

Personal Journal ✿

_____

_____

_____

_____ Date _____

Stage 7: The Void

Eventually, infinite consciousness will be seen for what it is, which is not peaceful, and which is dependent upon perception. When this realization hits home, your mind will quickly reject infinite consciousness, with an overwhelming feeling of nothingness prevailing. This is emptiness supreme; an absolute voidness that you will perceive as ultimate peace. Soon, you will be directing every bit of your attention to it.

DAY 211

Insight

It is coldest just before dawn.

Reflections

Can my worries and fears ever be replaced by something greater? Perhaps not—not unless I surrender them in my heart.

Meditation

Concentrate on the void.

Personal Journal

_____
_____
_____
_____ *Date* _____

DAY 212

Insight

Seeking enlightenment, I found nothing....Success!

Reflections

Until I die to my past and future, will I ever see the momentary brilliance? The problem is that I hold on doggedly to this past and future because everything I believe myself to be is there. I can't imagine what else exists.

Meditation

As your mind directs itself to this void, it thinks, *nothing is of consequence, everything is void.* It then yearns for solitude and seclusion, as it continually directs its attention to this void—directing...directing...until there is only the nothingness. The mind then rests there. Concentrate on nothingness.

Personal Journal

_____

_____

_____

_____ *Date* _____

DAY 213

Insight

Spirituality is a nasty word, a concept. Just see!

Reflections

Sometimes I seem to swap one delusion for another. Why shouldn't I? I have been deluding myself for years and I'm accustomed to it.

Meditation

The mind rests but it doesn't rest. One more step seems necessary but the mind isn't interested in taking it yet. The void is comforting. Concentrate on nothingness.

Personal Journal

_____
_____
_____
_____ *Date* _____

DAY 214

Insight

Truth tellers: forever alone, misunderstood by society.

Reflections

By constantly renouncing things that mislead me, by really turning my back on them regardless of the consequences, I begin to sift through the illusions that hold me captive. Even after this process, however, it is still difficult to let go. My instincts abhor loneliness, and therefore I search out companionship. At some point, however, mustn't I challenge this desperate loneliness, which leads to so much of my conflict, and experience being alone with my emotions restrained? This would be strong and mature; a solitude without my *self* involved.

Meditation

Here your mind clearly sees space as void. It also sees consciousness as void, and itself as void as well. Even at this lofty stage, however, there remains a degree of uncertainty that shows itself as only an intuitive feeling—but don't think about this uncertainty now. When the time is right, the reason for the uncertainty will become apparent. Continue to concentrate on nothingness for now.

Personal Journal

_____
_____
_____
_____ *Date* _____

DAY 215

Insight

Hide once and you will run forever.

Reflections

I need to experiment with fear. If I fear loneliness, I should isolate myself and then study my loneliness relentlessly. After this, there is an outside chance that I might never be lonely again.

Meditation

Your skills should be sharp by now. When you direct your mind to nothingness, it should be able to stay there as long as you wish. Stay with the void until your mind sees something more secure. Continue to concentrate on nothingness.

Personal Journal

_____

_____

_____

_____ Date _____

DAY 216

Insight

How could you not notice the full moon last night?

Reflections

I keep extremely busy. What am I running from? What horrible thing would happen if, for one day, I did nothing? Would I be wasting my time? The idea that I must get somewhere might be the one thing preventing me from getting *nowhere*.

Meditation

A feeling of non-existence results when you realize everything that has arisen in the past is now gone, including the last moment. Simply nothing exists! This poses no problem because of the incredible peace that results, but there is still an underlying feeling of suspicion. Continue, however, to concentrate on nothingness.

Personal Journal

_____

_____

_____

_____ *Date* _____

Stage 8: Neither Perception nor Non-perception

Your suspicions now become disturbingly real, as the void increasingly reveals itself as no different from the other immaterial experiences of boundless space and consciousness. Is it dependent upon something? This *something* is perception. Your misgiving grows ever stronger about the void until one day, your mind suddenly wakes to the realization that as long as there is perception, there cannot be total peace. Immediately after this insight, you will fall into the deepest state of concentration, when the state of "neither perception nor non-perception" is realized and then transcended, accompanied by the complete cessation of perception and feeling. Here, all mental unrest ends.

DAY 217

Insight

Don't shatter the blissful ignorance of those who refuse to see.

Reflections

Ignorance is bliss, they say, but my ignorance causes me great confusion, and when I do something while in this bewildered state of mind, things are never done well. Loose ends cause me endless entanglements.

Meditation

Concentrate on *neither perception nor non-perception.*

Personal Journal

_____
_____
_____
_____ *Date* _____

DAY 218

Insight

Accept everything, but watch carefully.

Reflections

It feels so aggressive to constantly fight the current. Should I accept my position in life and go from there? Live and let live? If I had a kind heart, I would concern myself with others now and not think so much about myself, but I can see that I can't do this consciously; it has to come from an acknowledgment that nothing exists in this one moment.

Meditation

This state of *neither perception nor non-perception* can only be described as light-years away from your other three immaterial attainments. Explanations are inadequate, but here your mind dwells in a state of non-attainment, non-desire, nonexistence—and yet somehow continues to function and register. The thought of a separate, individual mind is now inconceivable and seen as a fundamental misunderstanding. Nothing is truly left to lose now. Continue to concentrate on *neither perception nor non-perception*.

Personal Journal

_____
_____
_____
_____ *Date* _____

DAY 219

Insight

Cause no grief. Benefit everybody.

Reflections

I am becoming sensitive to my every action and word, and it's becoming painfully apparent to me when I hurt people, or even make them anxious. I just refuse to do that anymore, regardless of the consequences to myself.

Meditation

This state of *neither perception nor non-perception* is the culmination of concentration. Your mind is steady, mindful, sharp, and unencumbered by any idea of a separate existence. This steadiness encourages you to proceed to your next step—mindfulness. The eight stages of concentration sharpen the sword, but a sword is useless until it cuts through. Continue to concentrate on *neither perception nor non-perception.*

Personal Journal

_____

_____

_____

_____ *Date* _____

DAY 220

Insight

Words are images, only hinting of *Its* nectar. You must actually taste it.

Reflections

This whole thing seems to involve going beyond limitations, the limitations I only place on myself.

Meditation

Soon, you will use your concentrated mind to further your wisdom by practicing mindfulness. But for now, step out of *neither perception nor non-perception*, and simply concentrate on your forehead center after your warm-up exercises. Breathe into it as you previously did with nose tip concentration and imagine it open, full of white light, and full of healing breath. Remain focused on your forehead center while doing your daily activities; it will be as if you are looking through this center at the world.

Personal Journal

_____
_____
_____
_____ *Date* _____

DAY 221

Insight

Convenience turns its back on compassion.

Reflections

When something unanticipated is thrown into my equation, it creates problems for me as I adapt to the changes. How else is it done?

Meditation

Concentrate on the area between and above your eyes during practice now. To keep from becoming addicted to the previous immaterial calm states that you have developed, work at both maintaining a calm mind but moving forward as well. These calm states of concentration made it possible for you to progress, but they will now hold you back if you are not astute. You are on a razor's edge. Again, when participating in daily life, keep focused on this forehead center while out and about, except when driving!

Personal Journal

_____
_____
_____
_____ Date _____

DAY 222

Insight

Chaos. What a powerful, creative force.

Reflections

I must find clever ways to move my practice into my life. Perhaps I'll begin by keeping my attention focused in my forehead center while waiting in line at the grocery store or at traffic lights. If I can remember to do this, maybe I can extend it by holding my attention there even during conversations. What new things will I be able to see?

Meditation

Concentrate on your forehead center after your warm-up exercises of three breaths and opening your seven centers. Continually keep your focus on this area during your daily activities as if you are constantly looking through this center at the world. When there is nothing to look at or nothing to do, simply dwell on the white light between your eyes.

Personal Journal

_____

_____

_____

_____ *Date* _____

The 7 Energy Centers

The seven centers that you have been opening to begin each practice session are connections to your spiritual essence. Keeping them open is of great benefit as you advance in practice, as each affects your body, mind, and spirit in different ways.

The three lower centers deal with our intelligence, emotions, and experiences of pleasant and unpleasant feelings. Our base center at the coccyx deals with greed for survival. The pubic area is connected to our delusions, sexual lust, and power. The solar plexus involves our hatred. The greed, delusion, and hatred of these three lower centers can be both subtle and gross in our lives, and if we habitually surrender to their pressures and influences, they eventually dominate us with little hope for our rising above them.

The three higher centers deal with spiritual matters and various levels of love. The middle center, or the heart center, constantly coordinates the desires and requirements of the bottom centers (which keep our bodies alive but cause untold problems as well) with the love of the upper centers, in order to maintain a balance between body, mind, and spirit. This middle center, the heart, can reflect either the lower centers by promoting lust, or the upper centers by promoting unconditional love. It depends on one's spiritual inclinations.

As you concentrate on these centers, make them the center of your focus without distraction. A word of caution: All centers must be balanced with each other and not worked on individually without first doing your daily seven-step exercise, and as always, the centers are to be closed after practice in the correct order, beginning with the base of the spine, and ending with the forehead.

DAY 223

Forehead

Forehead concentration might create bits and pieces of vague scenes from the distant past, almost from the perspective of an animal, insect, or plant—sometimes even a mineral. This is very mysterious and difficult to explain. You might see beautiful colors, landscapes of flowing and brilliant hues in the forms of flowers and designs, feelings of aloofness (not a cold, but a loving aloofness), accompanied by surrender, urging you back into life at new and wonderfully expansive levels. This center has the power to organize and translate one's spiritual understanding into comprehensible wisdom as well, so it has a teaching aspect. This center is connected to the pituitary gland and is a deep reddish-blue in color. This forehead area is the recommended center to be focused on during daily activities, as if you are constantly looking through this center at the world. When there is nothing to look at or nothing to do, simply dwell between the eyes.

Insight

The blind man asks only for a small window.

Reflections

When thoughts are quiet, sacredness becomes my underlying experience. That's as close as I can come to describing it. It's real; it's unchanging.

Meditation

Continue to concentrate on your forehead. It is common for this area to warm up or tingle when your concentration is steady.

Personal Journal

_____

_____

_____

_____ Date _____

DAY 224

Insight

The eye between the eyes opens into other worlds.

Reflections

I have noticed recently that my ability to control difficult situations seems enhanced; there's not so much personal involvement. I find myself standing back now, not getting into the middle of things. It is not a disinterest but definitely a feeling of detachment, improving my judgment and sharpening my timing.

Meditation

Continue with your forehead concentration for today's sessions, bathing it in white light and opening it.

Personal Journal

_____

_____

_____

_____ *Date* _____

DAY 225

Insight

Opening yourself, little by little, to forces unknown.

Reflections

I can't really explain meditation. I just know it is not of this world. These experiences could never have sprouted from my mind. It could never have even imagined them.

Meditation

Begin with your opening exercises. Then, for the remainder of the period use your throat center as your concentration object, bathing it in white light and opening it. But focus on your forehead center during your daily activities.

Personal Journal

_____

_____

_____

_____ Date _____

A Year to Enlightenment

DAY 226

Throat

This area can cure and prevent illness. It is also common to feel immense hopefulness here while at the same time developing a capacity to differentiate clearly between truth and untruth. In addition, there will be a marked falling away of worldly aspirations, along with possibly hearing voices when concentrating on this center. Many of the things you hear, however, might not be immediately understood because they are coming from places not connected to your memory, but in time, their insightful nature will become clearer. Your ears might also begin ringing with two audible tones, one high-pitched and one low and humming. This center is connected to the thyroid gland and is bluish-silver in color.

Insight

Joyfully, watch the throat with uncluttered thoughts. It cures.

Reflections

I have noticed a definite change since working with my seven centers. My life is now more balanced, with excesses diminishing while other areas grow. Clarity is beginning to develop as well.

Meditation

Concentrate on your throat, bathing it in white light and opening it.

Personal Journal

_____
_____
_____
_____ *Date* _____

DAY 227

Insight

Enlightenment is a one-way ticket.

Reflections

I can never go back to who I was or where I've been. I've changed, people have changed, places have changed…everything has changed. Whether things have changed physically or not, however, doesn't seem to matter much; it is their images in my mind that have changed. This is what my mind consists of and I must get past them if I ever expect to glimpse truth. My hometown seemed much smaller when I went back.

Meditation

Proceed with your opening exercises, then, for the remainder of the period, concentrate on your heart center, bathing it in white light and opening it.

Personal Journal

_____

_____

_____

_____ Date _____

DAY 228

Heart

This area increases your capacity to understand at very deep levels, and instills the passion to either kill or love. A certain kind of boldness, not a reckless one, but a type necessary to understand truth, will result from concentrating on this area. The heart can dive to the depths of the lower, base centers with tremendous power, which could possibly result in violence, or it can reach for the heavens toward the highest love. It is the doorway to both worlds. This center is green in color and is connected to the thymus.

Insight

The heart of a lion: courageous.

Reflections

It is interesting to watch children play. When I play with them, however, I play from an entirely different perspective than they do. They're in their own world. As I make my way toward enlightenment, I notice my relationships with friends and relatives changing. My feelings for them have now become more of an expansive love rather than a clinging attachment, and they sense a change in me. It confuses them.

Meditation

Concentrate again on your heart center, bathing it in white light and opening it.

Personal Journal

_____
_____
_____
_____ Date _____

DAY 229

Insight

Illness: the great teacher.

Reflections

Illness has a grounding quality about it. Not only has it changed my direction in life, but it has also affected my very moral fiber. It seems to me that illness skillfully illustrates the distinction between worldly and spiritual values, such that some see illness as a tragedy that ruins lives, while others see it as an opportunity to alter destinies.

Meditation

Begin with your opening exercises. Then, for the remainder of the period, concentrate on your solar plexus, bathing it in white light and opening it.

Personal Journal

_____
_____
_____
_____ *Date* _____

DAY 230

Solar Plexus

Attention to this area can result in passages to strange places, some seemingly from far away places, and the descriptions of which would be difficult to explain. A feeling of determination might also take place if you can get on the other side of the fear that this center is known for. This feeling of determination will convince you that you can only go forward with no chance of backsliding, and that any future problems will never again be considered as your personal difficulties. The solar plexus has a reputation to initiate dreams of liberation, and visions of flying through the air effortlessly, leaving you breathless, and wondering why you weren't always this free. Focusing on this center can reduce physical and mental pain as well as mystically acquaint you with the physical aspects of the body, but only if you transcend its fear aspect. This center is yellow and is connected to the pancreas.

Insight

Without understanding, mind and heart remain separate.

Reflections

Many times, I ask myself why I even exist. Can I ever actually arrive at a point at which I understand my own potential? Wait! I can see that these questions have disappeared already, only existing for a moment. Am I on to something? Is there nobody or nothing behind the questions? Suddenly, I feel a bit freer.

Meditation

Continue concentrating on your solar plexus, bathing it in white light and opening it.

Personal Journal

_____

_____

_____

_____ Date _____

DAY 231

Insight

The tide comes in, the tide goes out.

Reflections

The earth rolls to meet the sun every morning, with the sun barely moving at all. Do I move toward enlightenment, or does it move toward me? It always seems to be there, waiting patiently, and not too far away.

Meditation

Proceed with your opening exercises, and then for the remainder of the period concentrate on the pubic area, bathing it in white light and opening it.

Personal Journal

_____
_____
_____
_____ Date _____

DAY 232

Pubic Area

Sexual lust will slowly give way to empathy, patience, and mercy, as a result of working with this area. This center is associated with the testes and ovaries, and is orange, like the setting sun. As a reminder, all centers must be balanced with each other and not worked on individually without first following your daily, seven-step exercise.

Insight

Ponder your navel, end grasping.

Reflections

I'm noticing how careless ambitions in the past have adversely affected others—the ones who have been with me for a long time, the very ones I am closest to and that I harm because time is such a true revealer of intentions. Wouldn't it be nice to end this foolishness by simply focusing below my belly button?

Meditation

Concentrate on your pubic area again, bathing it in white light and opening it.

Personal Journal

_____

_____

_____

_____ *Date* _____

DAY 233

Insight

Her eyes, steady and calm, completely filled with an abundant, full emptiness.

Reflections

Truth remains hidden from me. Seeing things as they actually are is difficult. I am understandably frightened of emptiness and become angry when confronted by it. My guide is faced with the daunting task of easing my fear without compromising the truth.

Meditation

Proceed with your opening exercises, and for the remainder of the period concentrate on the base of your spine, bathing it in white light and opening it.

Personal Journal

_____

_____

_____

_____ *Date* _____

DAY 234

Base of the Spine

This center at the base of your spine maintains your will to live. It is the foundation of physical energy. Concentrating on this center will relieve you of gluttony and greed, and because it is the foundation of fear, which collects in the other three lower centers, particularly the solar plexus, opening it will relieve tension and stress. The color of this center is fire red, mixed with orange, and is connected to the adrenal glands. This center, located in the coccyx area, lies alongside a potential energy that is asleep, waiting to be awakened. Many things, including meditation techniques, can awaken this force, and when it does become aroused, it will begin rising, opening each of the other centers until they all spin and whirl in celestial harmony as you meet your spiritual essence face to face!

Insight

Look through, not at.

Reflections

I make a path by walking the same way every day. It is a convenience, not having to make a new one each time I enter the forest, not having to consider which way to go. My life is overwhelmed with conveniences. What have I done with the immense amount of time I must have saved over the years? Perhaps conveniences and paths are suspect, blind to so many other possibilities in a measureless forest.

Meditation

Continue concentrating on the base of your spine, bathing it in white light and opening it.

Personal Journal

_____

_____

_____

_____ *Date* _____

DAY 235

Insight

She searched and searched for a teacher, finally finding herself.

Reflections

Aren't my teachers all around me? Where could I find a more profound teacher than right here in my heart? Haven't I always known the truth, but simply turned my back on it?

Meditation

Begin with your opening exercises, and then for the remainder of the period concentrate on your crown, an area about an inch or two above the top of your head. Bathe it in white light and open it.

Personal Journal

_____
_____
_____
_____ Date _____

DAY 236

Crown of the Head

This area is most stunning, sometime displaying a light orchid splendor surrounded by radiant white energy tinged with gold, flowing and vibrating at intense levels of activity. You will immediately recognize that this area, in particular, communicates with your spiritual essence. It is the report card of how well you are doing in your spiritual quest. This center is truly the doorway to enlightenment, approachable after the other six centers have been opened. This center is connected to the pituitary and pineal glands.

Insight

Let your stress flow out, over the top.

Reflections

These spiritual centers seem to beg for my attention, different ones at different times. When I feel attracted to one, I concentrate on it until the feeling subsides. It's as if they are reminding me of what needs balanced in my practice, and in my life.

Meditation

Concentrate just above your crown again.

Personal Journal

_____

_____

_____

_____ Date _____

DAY 237

Insight

Happiness will do for now.

Reflections

My disappointments grow from seeds of expectation. These expectations prove to be unrealistic, however, because they depend on a narrow happiness, the only kind of happiness that worldly existence offers—a surface happiness. I realize that meditators must endure disappointments, too, but these are extraordinary kinds of disappointments that work toward eventually ending all disappointment forever, resulting not in a mere surface happiness, but in the deepest, most satisfying contentment imaginable. Every moment, I make a choice of either going inward toward spirit, or outward toward the world.

Meditation

Return to your preliminary exercises of the three breaths and opening your centers. For the remainder of today's sessions, concentrate on your forehead center.

Personal Journal

_____

_____

_____

_____ Date _____

DAY 238

Insight

Truth initially stings more than it delights.

Reflections

Isn't truth better than uncertainty? I hate to discover a lie because of the disappointment I feel. This dismay, however, is quickly replaced by vindication, because now I have evidence of something I always suspected, but was afraid to confront, and now I'm finally released. As I surrender my delusions to truth, I come face to face with the emptiness of my life. This is always painful, but it's my destiny to know and not be deceived. Someday, I'll become cornered where the truth can no longer be ignored, and if I try to close my ears at this late date, a giant hammer couldn't batter me as hard as the truth will. But if I can uncover truth gradually, exposing myself to only small increments of pain, and never more than I can handle at any given time, then my delusions will be dismantled gently, piece by piece, so it will be tolerable both now and at the end. As a meditator, I understand this, and because of this unbelievable quest, nothing else satisfies me except this steady uncovering of truth, as painful as it might be.

Meditation

Continue focusing on your forehead. Soon, you will use your sharpened concentration to cut through your illusions with serious mindfulness. This will take courage.

Personal Journal

_____

_____

_____

_____ *Date* _____

DAY 239

Insight

Accumulations become heavy.

Reflections

I must solve a perplexing puzzle: How can this deeper happiness, which is initially depressing, ultimately free me? In addition, why is it that this surface happiness, so delightful at first, eventually binds me? I'll admit that no matter how much worldly happiness I experience, it is destined to disappoint me, sometimes not until the very end, but, alas, a lifetime passes as swiftly as a flash of lightning. On the other hand, this deeper happiness only increases as I slowly lose interest in playthings, leaving them behind like a growing child. Every spiritual advance requires a worldly surrender. This is how I find it to be, and my guide would not mislead me here.

Meditation

Continue to concentrate intensely on your forehead.

Personal Journal

_____

_____

_____

_____ Date _____

Part II: Mindfulness

Body

Concentration calms the mind, but concentration alone will not grant the freedom you are looking for. Concentration is crucial in establishing the next step, but something needs to stir up the calm mind that you have developed, such as stirring up the mud on the bottom of a pond, so that you don't become confused and believe that the mud is no longer there. This unique type of investigation, called mindfulness, is most effectively accomplished immediately after coming out of "fixed concentration," which is that full, bright calm that is experienced during practice when your meditation object disappears and after the visions and voices of "threshold concentration" cease. It is exactly when you come out of this fixed concentration that the mind is sharpest and can penetrate most easily from a metaphysical perspective into whatever is being investigated. This is called discernment, which leads to wisdom—seeing reality rather than images. These investigations into the body and mind will deepen as your meditation becomes an ongoing process, that is, continuously all day long.

This mindfulness is the second step leading to final insight, and is only successful when accompanied by an extremely concentrated mind, which is what you have been working on. Remember: It is necessary to integrate into your life whatever wisdom you discover. A good way to accomplish this is to take one step forward and then a half-step backward, so that you are certain of your progress. Be mindful of everything in this manner, and whatever wisdom does result, be careful that you don't cling to it, always allowing yourself to go on. We will begin with the body.

DAY 240

Insight

Body and mind: a short rope fraying on both ends.

Reflections

My body and mind are disposable, similar to napkins—use them once and out they go! So why become enamored with them? Perhaps my spiritual essence is only using them as a ship I must temporarily sail to gain wisdom and understanding.

Meditation

After your preliminary exercises, visualize your body, over and over, beginning with the tips of your toes and ending with the top of your head, inch by inch. Don't forget to visualize the insides, too—especially the insides!

Personal Journal

_____

_____

_____

_____ Date _____

DAY 241

Insight

Continuance is as certain as death.

Reflections

I'm afraid that this mindfulness will involve looking at things I normally abhor—my personal death and the distasteful parts of my body. I find it extremely difficult to look at myself in this manner because I identify so closely with my body. I can barely stand the sight of blood, I hate funerals, and I fall apart at the scene of an accident. My body seems to be everything I have, so it is threatening to observe it too closely. It is frightening to look at any of my delusions, too, but until I see through them, how can I be free to go on? The sooner I get past this idea that this body is me, the better. Thoughts are not me, the body is not me; so what am I?

Meditation

Resume your forehead center concentration. Mindfulness must walk hand-in-hand with concentration—it is a partnership. Always keep your concentration skills at their sharpest during any mindfulness practice; it is the only way to penetrate.

Personal Journal

_____

_____

_____

_____ *Date* _____

DAY 242

Insight

Never look closely, unless you want to see....

Reflections

Already I can see that this body of mine contains animal-like things! Teeth, skin, fingernails and toenails, body hair and head hair. But I don't consider myself an animal! I regard these things as beautiful—my beautiful hair and nails—but when they drop off, what's more disgusting than nail clippings on the floor, or a hair in my soup, or perhaps a week-old, decaying animal lying along the roadside? I must now be responsible and courageous, however, investigating to see the actual truth of this body I hold so dear. Hmm, let's see...my body is nothing but soft tissue and a skeleton, nothing substantial here, nothing to fall in love with. I don't seem to go any further than this bone in my arm!

Meditation

After your warm-up exercises, investigate your body again. Visualize it changing from an infant to an adolescent, then to middle age and eventually slipping into old age. From a baby's bald head to the full vibrant hair of a young woman, to hair that is thinning and losing its luster, and finally to graying hair before you become bald again. Slowly watch the changes take place, backward and forward in your mind, for your entire practice sessions. Imagine each part of your body changing from youth to old age—your legs, hands, face, and hair.

Personal Journal

_____

_____

_____

_____ *Date* _____

DAY 243

Insight

Blinded by the storm, I sought shelter where I could find it.

Reflections

Underneath this bag of skin covering my belly are many strange things: a tube from my mouth leading down to a pouch of undigested food, and further down, more tubes with waste products. Everything is coming and going, in and out. A bellows pushes air back and forth while a pump circulates blood. Looking directly at these things shouldn't alarm me, nor should I be disgusted by them, because this is what I am; this is where my spiritual essence decided to establish residency this time around.

Meditation

Forehead concentration is what you return to now. Mindfulness practice must await future sessions, but that shouldn't stop you from being mindful and aware of every activity in life.

Personal Journal

_____

_____

_____

_____ Date _____

DAY 244

Insight

The illusory self, how warm and fuzzy.

Reflections

I can't count on my body; it doesn't obey me. It merrily goes about its business without my direction, and in the end, it will dissolve into the elements and disappear without my approval as well. It doesn't follow my schedule; it follows its own schedule. My body is reminiscent of a comfortable house built near a raging river where I must live, knowing well enough that a flood could wash it away at any moment. It would be foolish not to consider escape routes when living in a house threatened with disaster, because when the time comes to leave, how would I be ready to get out in time? Therefore, because I can't rely on my impermanent body, shouldn't I invest in something I can trust, something that will be there for me when my body fails, which is not long from now, as it is beginning to rain, and the water is rising.

Meditation

After your preliminary exercises, envision your body lying in a forest, quite dead. Watch it slowly decompose, turning to dust in the sun and then melting into the ground with the rains—with nothing left but the undisturbed forest floor. Keep this in mind constantly during your sessions today.

Personal Journal

_____

_____

_____

_____ Date _____

DAY 245

Insight

Fall asleep consciously. Watch little dreams flash by before the nothingness.

Reflections

It seems to be in my best interest to develop my concentration to the highest degree possible, but without becoming attached to it. If I become attached, which is easy to do because of the peace it instills, I will undoubtedly be hesitant to move forward with my work of mindfulness. I can see, reluctantly, that mindfulness is crucial if I'm ever to acquire that unique, refined wisdom that will free me.

Meditation

Your calm, concentrated mind aids and supports your development of wisdom, and the extent to which it aids that wisdom depends on the strength of your concentration. Your concentration, like anything else, can be good, bad, or indifferent, and will promote wisdom that is likewise strong, weak, or middling. Return to your forehead concentration now. Don't be alarmed if you feel as if your body is beginning to separate from you at times, with the body over there and you over here, where you are merely keeping it fed and happy as if you were its custodian.

Personal Journal

_____

_____

_____

_____ $\mathcal{D}_{ate}$ _____

DAY 246

Insight

In every nook and cranny, we find these three: impermanence, discontent, and no underlying reality.

Reflections

It has been so long since I have completely trusted anybody. Mutual trust is everything in a relationship. With trust, every obstacle can be overcome and each can be secure in his or her feelings as both people work, uninhibited, toward a common goal. Without trust, I am forced to selfishly fend for myself as I lose the vulnerability and simplicity of love. Everything falls apart when that trust is violated and nothing is ever the same. Part of my investigation is determining how much I can trust this body and mind. I must be ever watchful of how they trick me.

Meditation

Continue with your intuitive mindfulness. Visualize your body without bones, poured into a bucket. A bucket of slush! Picture your body after its water has evaporated. An urn of dust! Then take some of the dust in your hand and blow it away. What's left? Contemplate these things today.

Personal Journal

_____

_____

_____

_____ *Date* _____

DAY 247

Insight

Relax. You are enlightened—you just don't know it yet.

Reflections

My guide tries to describe things that I have no capacity to understand. I lead a dim existence in a dark, dreary cave. Outside, many wondrous things exist, things I have no conception of, and things that could change my entire destiny. So what's holding me back from simply walking out of my cave and into the sunlight? At some point, I must be willing to change drastically and irrevocably, regardless of the consequences.

Meditation

Return to forehead concentration now.

Personal Journal

_____
_____
_____
_____ *Date* _____

DAY 248

Insight

The wealthy plan to leave their gold at heaven's gates, but no gold is found there.

Reflections

How should I live my life? Can I consciously accumulate wealth for myself when there is so much need in the world? I don't think I can do that. Perhaps I will live my life surrounded with love instead of riches and fame, and see for myself which is the greatest treasure.

Meditation

Without mindfulness, concentration is a sharp sword that never cuts anything; it is never given the opportunity to cut through your delusions. During your sessions today, consider your personal death, and whether you are prepared to die at any moment. Why couldn't you die right now, to your desires and ambitions, your worries and fears? Could you let go of memories, of security, and self-identity, coming up empty, dying to everything you are familiar with without fearing tomorrow? Without dying to these things, will you ever be free enough to feel real love—not attachment or lust, but real, unconditional, universal love, a love that doesn't depend on any love in return?

Personal Journal

_____

_____

_____

_____ $\mathcal{D}_{ate}$ _____

A Year to Enlightenment

DAY 249

Insight

Face fear straight away. Die one death only.

Reflections

I am discovering that fear is a good friend because it clears my mind. When I'm a hair's breadth away from oblivion, the fear erases everything. Only the sobering reality confronting me remains, as my insignificant concerns disappear into the reality of the moment. Just as an exercise, I think I'll spend a night alone in a dark alley, or in a cemetery, just to experiment with this fear.

Meditation

As you investigate your body, one area or aspect will become noticeably more interesting, perhaps your skin, hair, nails, or some organ. Keep the image of this part in your mind until the image drops into your heart. You will sense when this happens. It might take some time.

Personal Journal

_____
_____
_____
_____ Date _____

DAY 250

Mind

Where can you find your self inside your body? Are you inside your finger? Probably not, because if you lose your finger, you'll still be yourself. If you lose your arm, will you still be who you are? Yes; you will, because you are not merely your arm. What if your whole body disappeared except for your mind? Then where do you reside? You would still be you, wouldn't you? Then it's settled; your self must live in your mind, and this is where you must now look.

Insight

No self: frightening perhaps, but in a strange way, liberating.

Reflections

I noticed sadness in the faces I passed today while driving to work, and yet most will probably say that he or she is not suffering. It is such a big step to admit only that.

Meditation

Because your spiritual essence cannot be found inside your body, is it in your mind? You will begin investigating this mind soon, but for now, go back to your regular forehead concentration to sharpen your awareness. Only a trained mind can observe itself dispassionately. Look through the forehead during daily life.

Personal Journal

_____

_____

_____

_____ Date _____

DAY 251

Contact

Physically look at something. Notice that three things are involved: your physical eye, whatever you are looking at, and eye consciousness. These three things, your eye, the object, and consciousness, create a contact or sensation. Investigate that split second when your eye makes contact, and how this contact impacts your mind. Is the consciousness of your eye only present while it is looking, or is it always there? How quickly does the mind categorize the object and decide if it likes it or not?

Insight

Caught up in existence.

Reflections

So, how does my mind work? I'm going to look closely....Actually, it seems to work quite simply, very repetitively. When I see something I want, I get desperate urges. Then I somehow obtain it, and enjoy it, remembering the experience and perhaps wanting more! But when I see, hear, taste, think, feel, or smell something that I *don't* desire, then I push it away, never wanting to experience it again. I remember this, too. When I can't get what I want, or can't get rid of what I don't want, then the mind reacts, sometimes aggressively. And I find myself acting either from greed, anger, and confusion, or from generosity, kindness, and clarity. But what determines that?

Meditation

Begin with your warm-up exercises and then focus on your forehead center. Experiment with visual contacts during daily activities. Try to hold your attention at the moment of contact, before the mind identifies what it is looking at.

Personal Journal

_____

_____

_____

_____ Date _____

DAY 252

Insight

Fools create habits. Sages see nothing twice.

Reflections

Some urges and choices come from deep in my genes. They are derived from my accumulated, collective past. These reveal themselves as instincts, such that I'm automatically attracted to sweet smells, and disgusted by the smell of dung—attracted to the flower and wary of the snake. My past defines me. It accurately predicts my future, for what else could my reaction to the present moment be based upon other than my past?

Meditation

Resume your regular concentration today, beginning with your warm-up exercises and then focusing on your forehead center. Today, spend your entire sessions listening. Carefully notice how your mind reacts when you hear something. Again, try to discern whether ear consciousness is present always or whether it only arises upon hearing a sound. Try to hold your attention at that moment of contact, before the mind begins to identify the sound.

Personal Journal 🌹

_____

_____

_____

_____ *Date* _____

DAY 253

Insight

For one unbelievable moment, be truly free.

Reflections

I'm becoming suspicious of my unyielding opinions and judgments. They are, more often than not, based on unsubstantiated information—something I've read or heard from someone else, which I then accept as certainty without testing it, as if I am afraid to discover the truth about it. It then becomes a belief rather than wisdom. How can I ever hope to escape from this neverending wheel of what I am and what I've been if I just believe anything? Only when I test these things for myself will I someday see if eternity actually does exist in each moment. Then maybe I'll be able to interact with things without grabbing them or pushing them away, and just see them, without thinking about either acquiring or turning my back on them. If I can do this, then no future will be created by the present and the present won't be influenced by the past. Only the immediacy of this significant moment will exist, where everything is laid bare before me without deception. Am I truly a warrior?

Meditation

Resume your regular concentration today, beginning with your warm-up exercises and then focusing on your forehead center. During the day, practice by touching things. Notice how your mind perceives the feeling of touch, and observe what kinds of thoughts arise because of various touches. As you ponder the touching consciousness and how it arises, investigate whether a general consciousness fills the universe or whether each individual consciousness, your eye, ear, nose, tongue, body, and mind, arises and passes on its own. Try to hold your attention at that moment of contact, before the mind begins to identify the touch.

Personal Journal

_____

_____

_____

_____ Date _____

DAY 254

Insight

Time is but an illusion of consciousness. The moment is eternal.

Reflections

If only I could stop at the exact moment when one of my senses contacts something, and not proceed to the next step of attraction or rejection, then perhaps I would see the moment exactly as it is. To this end, I will try to use my memory and knowledge of the past wisely, only to acquire that which sustains me, but stopping at that point where I build a self inside of me. This false self always insists upon center stage, causing my countless conflicts by desiring things it doesn't have and pushing away things that plague it. This is the key to my troubles and discontent, this constant desire and obsessive wanting.

Meditation

Resume your regular concentration today, beginning with your warm-up exercises and then focusing on your forehead center. During the day, experiment with your sense of smell. Watch carefully how your mind reacts when you smell something, and how the smelling consciousness arises. Try to hold your attention at that moment of contact, before the mind begins to identify the smell.

Personal Journal

_____

_____

_____

_____ *Date* _____

DAY 255

Insight

Eat when hungry. Sleep when tired. That's it!

Reflections

I love food but I want to lose weight, so I quarrel with myself every time I walk past the doughnut shop. I want somebody's company, but she doesn't want mine, so I feel frustrated every time I see her. With these neverending disagreements, I'll always be out of harmony, at war with myself. How can I ever be whole? This internal bickering will only stop when I can remain in the moment, that exact moment when something contacts my mind—before my desires grasp at it or before my hatred runs away from it. How do I do this? It sounds so complicated. Actually, it could be very simple; maybe I only have to observe. But how do I observe without involvement? This is what meditation is about, teaching me to see in a radical way.

Meditation

Resume your regular concentration today, beginning with your warm-up exercises and then focusing on your forehead center. During the day, experiment with your sense of taste. Try holding your attention at that very moment of contact, before the mind begins to identify the flavor.

Personal Journal

_____

_____

_____

_____ *Date* _____

DAY 256

Insight

True creation is always spontaneous.

Reflections

Having concluded that my self is not located in my body, and therefore must reside in my mind, I investigated this mind and discovered something interesting. When something touches one of my sense organs, the organ's consciousness awakens with the contact. This happens the moment I initially taste, smell, touch, see, hear, or think something—just that first moment. One of three feelings toward the contact follows instantaneously: I will feel good (desire), bad (aversion), or neutral (indifference). This feeling is then immediately replaced by memory—my mind will attempt to recognize the contact from experience or, if it's a new contact, classify it and file it away for future use. Finally, imaginings and rambling thoughts will experiment with the memory of this contact, emotionally creating and constructing various ideas and plans. Therefore, my mind consists of only four uncomplicated aspects: an initial contact, then a feeling, then a memory, and finally rambling thoughts!

Meditation

Resume your regular concentration today, beginning with your warm-up exercises and then focusing on your forehead center. During the day, experiment with that first contact when something impacts a sense organ, that split second before any feelings arise toward it or any memories identify it. Try to hold your attention at that moment of contact, before the mind begins to sort it out.

Personal Journal

_____

_____

_____

_____ *Date* _____

DAY 257

Feeling

A contact is that particular instant when a sound touches your ear or a sight touches your eye. It lasts but a moment, followed immediately by a pleasant, an indifferent, or an unpleasant feeling. The pleasant feeling will bring up grasping, the unpleasant one will bring up aversion, and the neutral one will bring up indifference.

Insight

Feelings, like fireflies on a summer's eve. Blinking...blinking...gone.

Reflections

The mind operates through contact, feeling, then, a split-second later, memory, which takes over by categorizing the contact and storing the information. Initially there is contact with a sense object, followed by how I feel regarding this contact, then the memory identifies and stores everything—three steps. The fourth step is using my imagination and rambling thoughts to organize everything, transferring the initial contact into physical action, which involves emotions. I formulate a plan of action by constructing ways to grasp at and attach to desirable contacts and push away or avoid undesirable ones.

Meditation

Resume your regular concentration today, beginning with your warm-up exercises and then focusing on your forehead center. During the day, concentrate on the initial feeling—good, bad, or indifferent—that arises immediately after a sense organ contacts something.

Personal Journal

_____

_____

_____

_____ *Date* _____

DAY 258

Memory

When there is contact with one of your sense organs, watch carefully how your memory will quickly identify the contact if it is familiar, or classify it if unknown.

Insight

Sympathetic indifference is the reconciler of compassion and wisdom.

Reflections

Because these four—contact, feeling, memory, and rambling thoughts—arise and pass as independent sensations, where is a permanent self to be found in any of them? Am I in the initial contact? No, there is just the organ's consciousness that lies dormant until something touches it. But what if there was no contact? Then I must be in the initial feeling. But if there was no new contact, there would be no initial feeling, so where could I be? I must be in memory. Yes, here is where I finally can be found—in memory, but memory is no more than a record, filed in the recesses of my mind recording the past, so every bit of memory is dead. Memory, therefore, could not be me, because I am certainly not dead. That solves it! I must be rambling thoughts and imagination because this is the only thing remaining. But wait a minute. Rambling thoughts and imagination are based only on memory, and because memory is dead history, they must be dead as well. So...what am I?

Meditation

Resume your regular concentration today, beginning with your warm-up exercises and then focusing on your forehead center. During the day, investigate how your memory operates. Experiment with it.

Personal Journal

_____
_____
_____
_____ Date _____

DAY 259
Rambling Thoughts

Thoughts can happen before and after a sensory contact. Sometimes your eye will be directed to something at the command of a thought, for example, when you look at your wristwatch. At other times, you will see without seeing, as when you are driving and talking on a cell phone. Immediately after any sense contact, however, regardless of what prompts the contact, your rambling thoughts impulsively plan as a result of that contact. This is followed by emotion, will, and action. As you can see, cutting off any one of the four processes—contact, feeling, memory, or thought—will preclude action.

Insight

My self is gone; it is so quiet!

Reflections

Now I've run out of places for my self to hide. So, what am I, perhaps merely an imagination? The truth is what I must investigate—who or what am I? Once my heart is able to understand that my body is insubstantial and cannot be my self, then it will be easier to accept the possibility that my mind is also only so many arising and disappearing sensations, and cannot be my self as well.

Meditation

Resume your regular concentration, beginning with your warm-up exercises and then focusing on your forehead center. During the day, experiment with your rambling thoughts. Watch how they begin and then snowball into dramas.

Personal Journal

_____

_____

_____

_____ Date _____

3 Characteristics: Impermanence, No-self, and Discontent

If everything familiar to us in our world had three characteristics, what could they be? For one thing, we must consider if it is true that everything changes. Can we really hold on to the desirable things we chase after?

Then, are these desirable things exactly as they appear to be, or is there perhaps no underlying reality behind them? Are our bodies and minds permanent? Is there in fact an unchanging self, or is this self merely a creation of our minds?

Finally, we must think deeply about whether we escape our discomfort or increase it by compelling ourselves to chase after these desirable things.

We desire but we cannot possess because everything moves continuously, and even though we seek permanency and security in everything we do, it is not to be found. Our idea of permanency always results in disappointment because permanency is not a reality—it is an illusion, a dream, and when that dream is shattered time after time, we suffer. We discover that there is no underlying reality behind anything.

Understanding impermanence, no self or no underlying reality, and the resulting suffering, is the beginning of wisdom, for conditioned things cannot sustain a permanent integration. Thus, they are always tense, always shifting. This cannot be changed by anyone for there is no *self*, and therefore there is stress.

DAY 260

Insight

Impermanence, no-self, and discontent—a close observation of these three is the key.

Reflections

How can I closely look at these three characteristics: impermanence, no-self, and discontent?

Meditation

Try to understand and see for yourself how your mind, through thought, creates a self.

Personal Journal

_____

_____

_____

_____ *Date* _____

DAY 261

Impermanence

To investigate with mindfulness, initially we need to analyze two components: body and mind. Our body simply breaks down into chemicals, mostly water, and that's the extent of it. Our mind breaks down into four aspects: contact, feelings, memory, and imagination (rambling thoughts). These divisions of our bodies and minds are innocent in and of themselves. Only when we connect their various parts to create a self, do we become terribly confused. The truth is, every one of these aspects are obviously temporary, and this the first of the three characteristics of material existence—impermanence.

Insight

I just turned 40 when 60 sped by!

Reflections

I watch the various symbols arising in my mind—the little pictures and things, images of myself. These must be thoughts, too, initial thoughts, the previews before the movie and dialogue start. None of them lasts for more than a brief moment.

Meditation

All things in our universe are born and grow to maturity. Then they decline and fall apart as they make their way back to their original state. There is nothing in the material world that this law does not affect. Today during meditation, contemplate and investigate what can be found in your practice that doesn't decline. What is eternally there?

Personal Journal

_____

_____

_____

_____ Date _____

DAY 262

No-self

Even though these components of our bodies and minds are subject to change, we erroneously identify with them, attempting to make them permanent and seeing them mistakenly as ourselves. They are not ourselves, they are merely arising and passing occurrences. They must therefore be empty of a self, which is the second characteristic of material existence—no-self.

Insight

Self, built of sticks, fears the hurricane of truth.

Reflections

I cannot see my self no matter how intensely I try. I think that I know what it is, but I just can't grasp the illusion. It seems so real to me still.

Meditation

Contemplate the self within your mind.

Personal Journal

_____
_____
_____
_____ *Date* _____

DAY 263

Discontent

Once we create this false, insubstantial self, then it is necessary to protect, support, and agonize about it, as we would with any possession. Ultimately, we have no power over the impermanence of all things, and therefore find ourselves trapped with no real control, but with an imagined responsibility. This, of course, is a recipe for stress, which is the third characteristic of material existence—discontent. These three characteristics: impermanence, no-self, and discontent are, without a doubt, profoundly embedded in our bodies and minds.

Insight

Suffering: the primary great truth that must drop into the heart.

Reflections

I'm not discontented all of the time, but discontent lurks behind everything good in my life, constantly reminding me that something is amiss, as if I'm waiting for that other shoe to drop.

Meditation

Contemplate the displeasures that plague you. Look carefully. They are there.

Personal Journal

_____

_____

_____

_____ $\mathcal{D}_{ate}$ _____

A Year to Enlightenment

DAY 264

Insight

Pull your cloak close against the night's chill, but continue on your journey.

Reflections

I have investigated my mind, my body, and all their interesting parts, but I'm going to examine them again, only this time even deeper. I will scrutinize them in light of these three inherent characteristics: impermanence, no-self, and discontent. Only after I discover how these three characteristics interact with every part of my body and mind will my curiosity be satisfied.

Meditation

Concentrate on your forehead area today, always beginning your meditation with the preliminary exercises. Begin every session with these opening exercises, unless otherwise instructed, even when you're contemplating or investigating things. When out in daily life, as a practice, apply the three characteristics of impermanence, no-self, and discontent to everything you contact, both inside yourself and outside as well.

Personal Journal

_____
_____
_____
_____ Date _____

DAY 265

Insight

Go deeper in the valley.

Reflections

If I were to investigate the various aspects of my body and mind (contact, feelings, remembering, and imagination), in combination with the three characteristics (impermanence, no-self, and discontent), where would I begin? This sounds complicated, but perhaps it is not. Beginning with one aspect, for example my body, I'll combine it with one of the characteristics, for example, impermanence. I'll look at the impermanence of my body and observe how the body constantly changes. How long can I physically remain in one position before I need to move? How long before I must relieve myself, eat, or sleep? How many years does the body last? This body requires constant attention, and if I ignore it, there will certainly be discomfort.

Meditation

Continue with forehead concentration. The mind must be very refined for the mindfulness that lies ahead.

Personal Journal

_____

_____

_____

_____ Date _____

DAY 266

Insight

The only difference between life and death is the breath.

Reflections

Regardless of my undying attention and care, and even in spite of successfully curing my various illnesses and diseases, my body will disintegrate when it decides to, not necessarily when I'm ready. It would be prudent, therefore, to consider the impermanence of this body. I'll do this by looking directly at my body during practice, investigating it courageously from head to toe, repeatedly, inside and out, keeping in mind how everything about my body changes.

Meditation

After your preliminary exercises, contemplate the impermanence of your body.

Personal Journal

_____
_____
_____
_____ *Date* _____

DAY 267

Insight

Your spiritual essence is in front of time.

Reflections

If I thoroughly understand just one of these characteristics and its connection with only one of the aspects of my body or mind, maybe I'll automatically know every combination of the three characteristics (impermanence, no-self, and discontent) and the five aspects of body and mind, including contact, feeling, memory, and imagination. Then, I wouldn't be required to investigate each combination. I could choose the particular aspect/characteristic that interests me, and work with those two only. I could, for example, work on the impermanence of memory, trying to discover if each thought arises and disappears into a great nothingness where everything is apparently free and momentary with nothing and nobody behind it. By misunderstanding this impermanence, no-self, and discontent, I only confuse myself. Only by realizing that none of these characteristics and aspects are threatening in themselves, will I see them for what they are—simply constant movement. They only become burdens when I mistake them for my self, solidifying them and then tenaciously hanging on. Perhaps it is only thought that thinks.

Meditation

Practice deep forehead concentration.

Personal Journal 🌹

_____

_____

_____

_____ *Date* _____

A Year to Enlightenment

DAY 268

Insight

Let the mind touch nothing.

Reflections

Once my heart understands that these aspects and characteristics are blameless in themselves, I will be free to enjoy them. Why introduce desire, attachment, and clinging to my own body and mind, or other bodies and minds, when I can merely let things come and go in life no differently than allowing thoughts to rise and fall in meditation? This internal work of mindfulness is becoming so satisfying, creating tremendous energy. I feel as if my interest in this subject overshadows everything else! Actually, I can already see that no problems really exist in the world, for it is simply the world. The only problem is my misunderstanding and unrealistic expectations of life, and my misunderstanding of the aspects of the body and mind, seeing each of them as unchanging, substantial, and joy-producing, when in truth they are impermanent, unsubstantial, and the cause of discontent. I have a feeling that working with my misconceptions of the characteristics and aspects is the fuse that, when lit, eventually will clear up all of my confusion.

Meditation

Continue with deep forehead concentration today. Remember that anything you still value is locked in the mundane. Practice valuing nothing until valuing nothing becomes your natural state. Then you will have it all.

Personal Journal

_____

_____

_____

_____ Date _____

DAY 269

Insight

The reflections vary, but the mirror is eternal.

Reflections

There are three characteristics: impermanence, no-self, and discontent—and there is the body and the four aspects of mind: contact, feeling, memory, and thought. For my subjects of mindfulness study, I'll choose one characteristic and one aspect. Impermanence interests me as a characteristic, and memory strikes a chord as an ideal aspect for me to watch. So, I'm going to look at the combination of impermanence and memory—the impermanence of my memory.

Meditation

When investigating the combination of impermanence and memory, attempt to catch a thought when it first appears in your mind. Is it a picture? Is it a conversation or chattering? How long does it last before the next picture replaces it?

Personal Journal

_____

_____

_____

_____ Date _____

DAY 270

Insight

Mind. The king of magicians.

Reflections

During practice one day, a rather unusual, destiny-altering episode occurred. I detected thoughts blossoming, one after the other, in a corner of my mind. Each one initially appeared as a single frame but quickly developed into a story line, a dramatic movie. It might begin with a picture of myself sitting cross-legged and meditating, followed by the next picture, perhaps that of a friend. These two pictures were so fast that they created an illusion that the picture of myself was watching my friend. This went on in an endless sequence—pictures followed by memories, creating the illusion of a watcher observing the stories being created by my memory. I wondered, is this all I am—one thought following another in a continuous stream? Am I merely a series of pictures followed by the mind's memories of those pictures?

Meditation

Continue your mindfulness of mind pictures. When you mindfully investigate, don't think things through. Instead, place them in your mind and allow insight to arise.

Personal Journal

_____
_____
_____
_____ *Date* _____

DAY 271

Insight

Understand the "I" thought.

Reflections

In reality, there is only one thought following another. First a picture, then a memory, then another picture, then another memory, all creating a fictional observer. It is quite an illusion, a very clever trick, possibly the fundamental trick of my mind that builds a self or an "I" thought. I also noticed that it is impossible to think more than one thought at a time, even though their speed leads me to believe that many thoughts are occurring simultaneously. This illusion creates movies out of still frames and constructs an illusory watcher of thoughts. Without meditation, I could never have slowed my thoughts enough to discover this clever deception.

Meditation

Diligently continue to investigate the combination of one aspect and one characteristic.

Personal Journal

_____

_____

_____

_____ *Date* _____

DAY 272

Insight

Thoughts interrupting silence. Silence interrupting thoughts. What are interruptions?

Reflections

Is this all I am? A memory? In that case, what is there to lose...truly? Why should I fear death? What is it that will disappear, or rather who will disappear? Can something never existing in the first place, except in a fanciful imagination, cease to exist? How silly it is to regard myself with such importance, laughable actually, to realize that I'm simply a picture and a memory? What a tremendous relief! I mistakenly thought I was something tangible. For just the fraction of a moment, I glanced at the cessation of my existence. But even with these tremendous insights, my insatiable wants and desires remain. How can I take this wisdom into the depths of my heart and accept the fact that I'm nothing? How could something, concocted of a series of pictures and memories, survive anything, even the next second, let alone death? It must be this illusory self-memory that causes my "I" thought to roll along so merrily.

Meditation

Investigate the various characteristics and aspects, not only during your practice but in life as well. At your job, within relationships, and while doing what you love to do, see the impermanence, the absence of an underlying reality, and the seeds of discontent in all of material existence.

Personal Journal

_____

_____

_____

_____ _Date_ _____

DAY 273

Insight

Enlightenment is life, not merely the meaning of life.

Reflections

I feel my body breathing. I detect my organs working and pumping. But it is not me. I see my mind thinking. But it is not me. What am I, exactly? Am I truly my spiritual essence? Is this spiritual essence all of me? Because I have seen for myself that I don't exist in the way I had always thought I did, there is no recourse but to find my spiritual essence regardless of the difficulties, because this discovery is the key to my freedom. Beyond my personality and beyond my memory, which I have identified as my watcher, there seems to be something greater, something yet to be understood. This search for truth is an examination of everything, both physical and metaphysical. It requires a very concentrated, dedicated mind. This practice had been an act of faith so far, but now it's becoming an affirmation of something much greater than myself. What is it that has no beginning and never ends? Am I a part of something that is immortal? What is there to worry about...ever?

Meditation

Continue to investigate the three characteristics, as well as the body and the four aspects of mind.

Personal Journal

_____

_____

_____

_____ Date _____

DAY 274

Insight

Don't play with dead things.

Reflections

I am determined to get to the bottom of this impermanence, no-self, and discontent. I will scrutinize how these three characteristics affect my body and mind and discover how they imprison me. As of now, I am little more than a beast in a cave, held captive by my misunderstandings. At one time, I thought these aspects were me. Now I'm discovering they are merely rising and passing occurrences with nothing supporting them. I had always counted on this jumble of a physical body and mind to sustain me, but I'm realizing that the parts do not equal a whole. There is no whole, only a puppet with its many strings. There are simply impermanent parts, illusions that have become my prison.

Meditation

Keep at it, night and day, until you come to an understanding regarding your mind and its illusions. The bottom must drop out completely for true insight to take hold.

Personal Journal 🪷

_____

_____

_____

_____ $Date$ _____

DAY 275

Insight

Before eternity, It was there.

Reflections

So far, I have seen that thoughts are only thoughts; they are not me. Memories are mere memories; not me either. Pain is just pain; it is separate from me. The breathing during meditation—again, not me, nor is it being done by me. So who is me? Am I just the memory of a fleeting, momentary contact—that moment when a sight, a touch, a thought, a sound, a taste, a smell, appears? Is there only the passing sight or thought, followed by a memory that creates me, the illusory watcher? This illusion is too powerful to be understood without insight, let alone accepted, for only a very still mind, where all that enters is reflected like a great mirror, can embrace this truth. An extraordinary mind similar to this would be free from illusions, capable of understanding the way things are. There would be no self directing this reflection; everything would come and go without a trace. And when all of this is finally taken into the heart, that heart would be free within each moment, and each moment would be an eternity unto itself.

Meditation

Continue investigating the various characteristics and aspects. Don't forget to begin every session with your preliminary exercises.

Personal Journal

_____

_____

_____

_____ Date _____

DAY 276

Insight

Time requires consciousness.

Reflections

As I develop this mindfulness, it is easier to contradict everything—my conclusions, my desires, my pursuits—and, oddly enough, my search for enlightenment. I can turn my back on it because I see how even this quest keeps me imprisoned. My ideas and my learning, my history and my heritage, my hopes and my dreams—I discard it all. I now find myself rejecting old ideas of security, fear, attachments, and fond memories, as I continue this practice of concentration and mindfulness. I see my self slowly and imperceptibly slipping away, as my capacity to watch everything with clarity increases. It is as if I'm seeing for the first time, without the burden of stale impressions that had been burned into my memory.

Meditation

Continue investigating the various characteristics and aspects.

Personal Journal

_____

_____

_____

_____ *Date* _____

DAY 277

Insight

I looked deep into the well but saw no reflection.

Reflections

I'm ready to face that emptiness, the emptiness that was so frightening in the past and left me with no choice but to escape from it. I knew in my heart that I could never flee its truth, but still I turned my back on it even though emptiness was the only thing that could set me free. Now I'm ready to see it—not only see it, but to become it, knowing that until I become it, I will never accept it. This determination and resignation to see are the very things that will chain me to the emptiness, until I am forced to walk through its doorway toward my spiritual essence. In that indescribable moment when everything else is gone, I know that my being will be filled with light...and that there will be freedom, freedom in the form of inexpressible love within the immensity of eternity. Then, my self, as I've known it, my jailor, will suddenly vanish. The barriers between my experiences and the one who experiences will be dismantled, as I absorb into whatever appears in my field of consciousness. I'll truly understand the oneness of all things, and I will finally be free, free of myself, never to be shackled again.

Meditation

Resume forehead concentration now.

Personal Journal

_____

_____

_____

_____ Date _____

DAY 278

Insight

Travel with eyes wide open, courageously.

Reflections

In meditation, I can see that my thoughts and emotions are not my *self*. My body is not my *self* either, but this is more difficult to see. I understand it in my head when I see a dead body, but to understand it in my heart is another story. The only answer is to watch this body relentlessly, this "I" thought, until wisdom regarding it arises, for until this "I" thought falls away, I will surely cling to my personality as a fly clings to garbage. Thinking about the "I" thought will never dismantle it; I can only remain aware of it persistently as I continue my journey, waiting for the truth to drop into my heart. Occasionally, I just watch myself and surrender to the fact that I'll never change, and I stop trying. The sobering reality of my illusions then impresses me deeply.

Meditation

Concentrate on your forehead and begin extending your sessions in preparation for the next step. Visit a respected meditation center or monastery now, if possible. While you are there, you will be permitted to become a complete failure in the eyes of an ambitious world, as you work internally. Groups and teachers can at times be helpful, but don't lean on them too much or depend upon them for your progress. It always comes down to a solitary effort if authentic progress is to be made. A teacher's great insight is merely a reflection of your own potential, and each path is different as we weave our way to enlightenment.

Personal Journal

_____

_____

_____

_____ *Date* _____

DAY 279

Insight

When enemies know each other intimately, the weapons are set aside.

Reflections

I looked at my friend today, and surprisingly, I saw myself. It was a bit disquieting, but comforting as well. I'm sure this happens in different ways to different people, perhaps noticing that their hands are no different from another's, or that their thoughts and hopes are the same. Maybe this type of mutual identification with others is the only way that I will ever be able to love my neighbors. I can't love them from the outside looking in; it has to be a oneness, a forgiveness as such, forgiving myself and surrendering my arrogance. Only then will there be an authentic feeling of unconditional love.

Meditation

Continue with forehead concentration.

Personal Journal

_____

_____

_____

_____ _Date_ _____

DAY 280

Insight

Mind, trying to steer rudderless, free ships on an endless ocean.

Reflections

The mirror of my association with people and things reveals the depth of my spirituality. Only when I authentically regard both myself and my understanding to be no better than anyone else's will progress be made, but I seem to be getting nowhere lately. I am becoming restless and tired, and my whole life appears to have been a failure. My despair is bottomless and I don't really know where to turn. Both my life and my spiritual quest have lost their enchantment, and I am dead inside.

Meditation

Concentrate on the image that constantly arises in your mind—that image of your self.

Personal Journal

_____

_____

_____

_____ Date _____

DAY 281

Insight

I thought I saw myself dancing on the lake, but it was only the moon.

Reflections

I see beautiful sights, hear soft murmurings, and feel the touch of exquisite things. I smell delicious odors, taste luscious foods, and daydream endlessly. I was born with these hungry senses, and I accommodate them in every way, searching for pleasures and discriminating between likes and dislikes. I find security in numbers, form villages and countries, and defend them to the death. Money affords me the luxury to do what I desire instead of toiling at something I hate, so even though I mouth spirituality, economics becomes my religion. Then, to fend off loneliness, I procreate the species. Soon, my body dies, which is a good thing. Otherwise, the world would be full of people. So is that it? Is that all there is? As I look pleadingly to the heavens for answers, I realize that all of this has to do with me. Me, this self-centered anchor that holds me at port, never allowing my spiritual essence to sail the unfathomable seas.

Meditation

Contemplate the "I" thought. See if everything begins and ends with it. Get to know it intimately.

Personal Journal

_____
_____
_____
_____ Date _____

A Year to Enlightenment

DAY 282

Insight

It is so strange. Everything is gone.

Reflections

Without my body and mind, there is no existence as I know it. Life only happens while body and mind exist, and if there is nothing behind them, where is my self? I must continue in some way. This pleading question, this question right here, is my problem—this wanting to become something, to continue. How can something that has never existed continue? Suddenly, I feel as if I am now waiting for something to happen and can do nothing further myself, as if I have no more power and must rely on something else to carry me.

Meditation

Continue investigating the "I" thought.

Personal Journal

_____
_____
_____
_____ Date _____

DAY 283

Insight

When the "I" thought is gone, what remains?

Reflections

How can I expect to gain total freedom when I'm still intimidated? What is it that controls me? I try to find my controller by asking, but if I am nothing and simply disappear, what will happen to me? There! Right there in my question— I have found my intimidator. It is nothing more than my attachment to continuing existence. It is asking too much of me to let it all go with no assurances of what, if anything, will be on the other side.

Meditation

Just sit today. Don't contemplate or concentrate on anything. Whatever occurs, notice it, and then release it with kindness, compassion, and wisdom.

Personal Journal 🪷

_____

_____

_____

_____ *Date* _____

DAY 284

Insight

Fools desire existence. Sages merely breathe.

Reflections

I don't want to exist! With this said, my attachment to non-existence holds me back. I don't care what happens! Now, irresponsibility and an unwillingness to investigate life deeply delays me. Am I beginning to see the culprit here? "I, I, I." Doesn't it make me want to throw my self away at some point and just be?

Meditation

Just abide, with full awareness, with whatever presents itself. Put up no resistance. Stop doing now.

Personal Journal

_____
_____
_____
_____ *Date* _____

DAY 285

Insight

Continuity exists, but its character is unknowable.

Reflections

Can I influence my hereafter by what I do on earth? If whatever I perceive becomes my reality, then clinging to the idea of myself going to a hereafter is probably where I'll end up, for a while. But this whole question of destiny revolves around me—me, being an idea, an idea of my self. This is an important point, for if I can resolve this idea of self, wouldn't the fate of whatever it is that continues be entirely different?

Meditation

Resume concentration on the forehead center now.

Personal Journal

_____

_____

_____

_____ Date _____

DAY 286

Insight

Understanding leads to insight, insight to love, and love is the essence.

Reflections

Why was I born? A fair question. A better question might be, where was I before I was born? This is as important as asking, where will I go after I'm dead? What will I be? Because there can be no destruction of my spiritual essence, and because my essence is not me, and yet is a part of me, there can be no doubt that there will be a continuation. Wouldn't it be ironic if the quality of that continuation depended on nothing more than the depth of my understanding immediately before my body or mind shuts down?

Meditation

Stay with your forehead concentration today.

Personal Journal

_____

_____

_____

_____ *Date* _____

DAY 287

Insight

Whatever we spread covers us like a blanket.

Reflections

Perhaps only my intuitive understanding continues after death, not my knowledge. A vast chasm exists between the two. Perhaps I not only leave my body behind, but my personality and memories as well, with only my level of developed intuition determining what form I take in the next world. Although I might then be in a different form or body, I don't think I could escape what I've done in this world. I am certain I would feel the causes and effects of my conscious actions, because those actions would reflect the foundation of my understanding at the time those actions were committed. When the after-world arrives, I will feel the effects personally, no matter where or who I am, just as I am now personally experiencing the results of something that happened in the past and pushed me into this world. Until my understanding reaches beyond this "I," until enlightenment happens, this belief in myself might cause unending illusions in the many worlds that could lie ahead.

Meditation

Concentrate deeply on your forehead center.

Personal Journal

_____
_____
_____
_____ *Date* _____

DAY 288

Insight

Falling in love with enlightenment, not unlike worshipping a stone.

Reflections

I can always find something to latch on to. If it is not a person or possession, it will be an idea or a cause. It is not the infatuation as much as it is allaying my fear of an empty moment. Emptiness is so intimidating, leaving all hope behind. Yet, it is exactly this hope for myself that perpetuates this condition of dependence. How can I translate the word "hope," I am so intertwined with it and involved with the concept of a substantial, unchanging self. Hope represents strong desire, the root of my suffering according to the wise, and the antithesis of freedom. Wanting or hoping to achieve any state of mind—salvation, enlightenment, or anything else—represents a condition arising from a cause, an effort. If it is true that all conditioned things are transient, what could I desire that would be eternal? What could a transient being like myself know of eternity? I only mislead myself when I think that any state graspable by my mind can represent ultimate freedom. Do I really believe that the Source of all there is really thinks as I do, or is subject to the laws of physics, or knowingly creates? How egotistical of me to think on such a limited scale, as if I'm the center of the universe. What could an enlightened mind communicate to people like me that would be knowable?

Meditation

Maintain your deep forehead concentration.

Personal Journal

_____

_____

_____

_____ *Date* _____

DAY 289

Insight

Nothing lasts. The poor man runs out of money. The rich man runs out of life.

Reflections

Who am I, exactly? Or what am I? Do I have a great stake in myself? Maintaining my personality gets so bothersome at times. Why do I continually prop it up? What progress is possible if I endlessly seek to be other than what I am? Could it be that real progress starts with first facing my self, even before I can understand it?

Meditation

After your preliminary exercises, focus on your seven centers. If any area is particularly sensitive, or if your attention is drawn to it, concentrate on that center for the remainder of each session today.

Personal Journal

_____

_____

_____

_____ _Date_ _____

DAY 290

Insight

What's underneath?

Reflections

I'm feeling increasingly at home in nature. The wonderful thing about nature is its vastness. I can take in as much as I want and not diminish it. At this point, however, nature only appears as mountains, rocks, water, and trees. At one time, it was far more than that.

Meditation

Again, focus on the most sensitive of your seven centers.

Personal Journal

_____

_____

_____

_____ *Date* _____

Part II: Mindfulness

DAY 291

Insight

Rest within the hands of eternity.

Reflections

My momentary insights are mere flashes of creativity. Imagine my whole life being creative every moment with no old insights remembered, for old insights become nothing more than knowledge, information that gets tucked away in a book somewhere. Some might presume that they can become enlightened by just reading about these things, believing in them, and not doing the work required, but their conflict will not change. More clearly, every day, I can see how a life lived outside of these new insights can be so scattered. It is as if these preliminary insights are a tease, tempting me to go all the way and to become a completely harmonized being.

Meditation

Stay within your seven centers again. If no particular area attracts you, focus on your forehead.

Personal Journal

_____
_____
_____
_____ Date _____

DAY 292

Insight

What is it that practices meditation?

Reflections

Why am I so restless? I'm restless because I must stay ahead of emptiness. Distractions are paramount, more important than all the gold in the world because wealth is not what I crave. What I crave is the feeling that I'm real, that I'm accomplishing, that there is an underlying reality behind my activities. I long for the excitement of achievement, the realizing of a goal: "I" am, "I" do, "I" accomplish. These things, whether harmful or beneficial, create the "I," which must then be protected and defended, creating excitement, but fear as well, and destroying any possibility of love. When the action finally stops, perhaps voluntarily through meditation, or perhaps unwillingly by natural causes, the emptiness I have avoided for so long looms ominously. I am suddenly faced with the reality of impermanence and shifting sands as my past washes over me again and again. This insecurity causes great alarm, an apprehension that only intensifies when I further discover that there is no fundamental reality behind anything. I would be extremely foolish to wait for my last breath to face all of this.

Meditation

Continue working on your seven centers. If no particular area attracts you, focus on your forehead.

Personal Journal

_____

_____

_____

_____ _Date_ _____

DAY 293

Insight

Still caught in our subtle prison of desires.

Reflections

I have now exhausted every possible escape. Fame, wealth, power, religion, spirituality—none of them worked as I continue to search for happiness. I don't desire merely a happy experience; I want constant, unending happiness. I want, I want, and I want some more! I had already experienced happiness in my early days of practice, but I wasn't satisfied. I still needed more happiness, with increasingly more exquisite feelings in the future. With my insatiable wants and desires, how can I stay in this moment where truth is to be found? When will I ever stop doing and wanting, and simply be?

Meditation

After your preliminary exercises, sit quietly with no agenda whatsoever. Stay unswervingly within each moment. Movement is the nature of the body and thoughts are its engine. Behind these movements however, is nothing. This is how movement and thought should now be approached, each merely a phenomenon of nature, each being the result of a previous cause, and all collectively the continuous cycle of illusions.

Personal Journal

_____

_____

_____

_____ Date _____

10 Obstacles of Enlightenment

How will we know when we're enlightened? We will know that the process has begun in earnest when we overcome three things: our belief in an eternal personality, belief that dogma or rituals can replace the hard work of seeing through our illusions, and doubt and skepticism that total liberation is possible. Then the process deepens with two additional serious obstacles: lustful sense desires and anger are weakened. Then, the process deepens once more when these two obstacles are vanquished completely. The process is completed when we overcome five additional obstructions: attachment to form realms, attachment to formless realms, self-righteousness, agitation, and our ignorance of the basis of humankind's dilemma, which is the "I" thought, as well as our ignorance of the solution to that dilemma. These 10 obstacles can become subtle and operate at refined levels, but they must be defeated.

DAY 294

Insight

I can do nothing else.

Reflections

In my practice, I have seen happiness as a delight, as merely an emotion that comes and goes. Why would I want to become attached to such a thing that's not stable? Happiness is fully experienced in the exact moment it arises, never to be possessed, and desiring its continuance is far removed from its truth. So, if not for happiness, for what reason do I still seek enlightenment? My guide is waiting for an answer; I'd better be quick about it!

Meditation

Today, keep your mind open and bright, but decisive in reflecting everything back to its source. The moment you notice a contact with a sense organ, return the contact to its source. Notice the sensation of hearing, not the sound heard; the awareness of seeing, not the object seen. This split-second of awareness should be applied directly at that point of contact without allowing the mind to identify, judge, or think about the object.

Personal Journal

_____
_____
_____
_____ *Date* _____

DAY 295

Insight

Fools take a name; gain some fame. Wise ones gain nothing.

Reflections

The first question is, will my personality remain unchanged in the next world, as if my body and mind will just float up to heaven? This I must contemplate to gain further wisdom.

Meditation

After your preliminary exercises, leave yourself completely empty.

Personal Journal

_____
_____
_____
_____ _Date_ _____

DAY 296

Insight

My church, a grove of aspen. My God...infuses me.

Reflections

Will rote memorization of teachings and acting out of rituals ever bring me face to face with my spiritual essence? Won't this momentous meeting require a deeper mindfulness, a true, intuitive understanding of what I am? What separates me from my great Source?

Meditation

Concentrate on your forehead.

Personal Journal

_____

_____

_____

_____ *Date* _____

A Year to Enlightenment

DAY 297

Insight

Questions are more important than answers.

Reflections

How can I rid myself of unending doubt? Perhaps the only way to conquer doubt is to see concrete results in my practice—I have to prove things true for me. At some point, I know that doubt must be overcome. If it isn't, there will be little resulting insight.

Meditation

Simply watch every natural movement of your breath today.

Personal Journal

_____

_____

_____

_____ _Date_ _____

DAY 298

Insight

Equanimity and tranquility share no bed with indifference.

Reflections

Anger and ill will toward others, especially those with differing viewpoints, are huge obstacles standing in the way of my hopes for enlightenment. Spirituality is too sensitive to endure these types of strong emotions. I must stand on a small arched bridge over a tranquil Japanese garden and view my adversaries as lotus blossoms floating in the pond.

Meditation

Ponder the emptiness of the moment and experience its incredible fullness.

Personal Journal

_____

_____

_____

_____ Date _____

DAY 299

Insight

Drifting off to dreamless sleep, I caused no undue pain today.

Reflections

Sense-based desires surely divert my attention from enlightenment. When I crave things, things that delight my eye, please my ear, smell good to my nose, taste wonderful to my tongue, feel exquisite to my touch, or bring pleasure to my mind in imaginations and memories, then I will be misdirected in my quest. If I come across these delights by chance, I will enjoy them to the fullest! However, if I then crave them, wanting more and attempting to turn them into pleasures, then they will deceive me in my mission.

Meditation

Stay within emptiness now during your practice. Visualize your cushion empty—you are no longer there. Stay with the image of that empty cushion for both of your sessions today, replacing the normal image of yourself that usually comes to mind.

Personal Journal

_____

_____

_____

_____ *Date* _____

DAY 300

Insight

Don't hesitate now.

Reflections

I hope in my next life I will have a form. Does hoping for this, however, curse me with the lingering illusion of a separate self? I must look carefully at this.

Meditation

During practice today, remain within the great void of eternity, within emptiness.

Personal Journal

_____

_____

_____

_____ $\mathcal{D}_{ate}$ _____

DAY 301

Insight

Do what is necessary; leave the rest undone.

Reflections

Hoping that in the next world I would in some way be formless so that I could be peaceful is still deceptive, a dualistic idea of an individual self. Again, this must be contemplated.

Meditation

After your preliminary exercises today, notice your persistent desire and hope to experience something new during practice.

Personal Journal

_____
_____
_____
_____ Date _____

DAY 302

Insight

Only say what is necessary.

Reflections

If I become proud and conceited regarding my understanding of spiritual matters, thinking that I know, thinking that my understanding is far superior to others, thinking that I have attained, then I'll never reach enlightenment. What could I ever know that would be more than a grain of sand from the limitless beaches of my Source?

Meditation

Take your practice beyond the moment and beyond emptiness today. Take it further than you have ever gone.

Personal Journal

_____

_____

_____

_____ *Date* _____

Insight

Sifting through the ashes of our perceptions; looking for truth.

Reflections

If my mind is confused, restless, and distracted, opposed to clarity and far from insight, I will never reach my goal. I will live within the prison of my knowledge, never in the spontaneity of the moment, pushing my beliefs on others and becoming nothing more than an ambitious, political force.

Meditation

For the next few sessions, don't do anything, not even your preliminary exercises. Just sit quietly. Other than maintaining a bright awareness of everything arising, try not to control anything. You are a spectator with no agenda, but aware of every arising.

Personal Journal

_____

_____

_____

_____ *Date* _____

DAY 304

Insight

Wherever it takes you, be true to yourself.

Reflections

Ignorance goes far deeper than just egoism and personality. It is a belief that I will always be a separate entity looking forward to eternal experiences, set well apart from my spiritual essence, thinking that the spiritual essence is merely a part of an immortal me. It means that I remain ignorant of the basic truth that all beings suffer, and even when I find what alleviates the suffering, I cling and attach to it. This only causes the suffering to increase. But it is the me that is the illusion, as my practice has shown.

Meditation

Just sitting now, no direction, no goal, no understanding. All that remains is a bright, piercing mind as everything is forgotten—no plans, no regrets— only this exquisite moment.

Personal Journal

_____

_____

_____

_____ _Date_ _____

DAY 305

Insight

Those who foolishly live for themselves die likewise, many times over.

Reflections

I know, without a doubt, that I am selfish. In a very subtle sense, everything revolves around me. Every thought is connected to me, and if I'm not constantly the celebrity of my small, private world, I'm miserable. When others try to elbow into this personal space, I fight them off and consider them threats because I am so selfish about my little world. I must always be the center of attention in my mind.

Meditation

Whatever appears in the mind, know it, and release it.

Personal Journal

_____

_____

_____

_____ $\mathcal{D}ate$ _____

DAY 306

Insight

Intentions are always suspect. Go beyond intentions; look deeper.

Reflections

When I'm considerate of others, helping them in some small way, I am still in the center of that thought, scheming how I'll personally benefit. Perhaps I want to feel good about myself, or needed—or maybe conspire to improve my meditation by being compassionate. This thinking primarily of me is a basic, deep-seated greed. I always want things to go my way. This must be resolved or I'll never get beyond this false idea that my self is central to everything, and I'll stay mired in my delusions regardless of if they are worldly or spiritual.

Meditation

Direct your attention to nothing in particular, and with no concern regarding results. Do only what needs to be done in this particular moment.

Personal Journal

_____

_____

_____

_____ _Date_ _____

DAY 307

Insight

The sun is out but I have no shadow. How strange.

Reflections

This fixation with myself never changes. Even though I am aware of the obsession, as very few are I suppose, I still can't see it. It permeates my being similar to a terrible stench causing undue conflict and discontent because of the heavy responsibility I subtly feel toward the welfare of this imaginary me. If I don't find a way to overcome this addiction, my heart will bleed forever. I'm just not ready yet to make the drastic changes I know are required.

Meditation

Return to forehead concentration today.

Personal Journal

_____
_____
_____
_____ *Date* _____

DAY 308

Insight

A fox guards the chicken coup, a mind searches for enlightenment.

Reflections

Trying to change this "I" thought requires altering something very ingrained and precious—the most precious possession I have. It involves the demystifying of myself. This is necessary because this "I," this me, is intermingled with my every thought and emotion. I can never put aside this "I" thought by trying to do it directly because the "I" thought would be the very one making the attempt, and therefore strengthening itself by the effort. My difficulty in finding enlightenment is that the one looking for it is the one who must disappear. What a predicament!

Meditation

Continue with forehead concentration.

Personal Journal

_____

_____

_____

_____ Date _____

DAY 309

Insight

The moon, my only friend now, came to visit again last night.

Reflections

The most effective thing I can do is notice and release the "I" thoughts carefully during meditation. Three things I must be constantly aware of: the "I" thought, emptiness, and the moment. These seem to be the crucial elements of developing insight.

Meditation

For today's sessions, investigate emptiness.

Personal Journal

_____
_____
_____
_____ *Date* _____

DAY 310

Insight

Peeling onions, tears well up.

Reflections

I have become acquainted with my mind by allowing thoughts to dissolve rather than following them. It is this knowing, this awareness that the mind is in the process of thinking, rather than allowing thoughts to run wild, that separates meditation from normal mental activity. Then I delve even deeper and know the one who is aware that I am thinking. Then I look for the one who is aware that I am aware of the one who is thinking, and it goes on and on, deeper and deeper, uncovering layer upon layer.

Meditation

Resume your preliminary exercises now and then concentrate on your forehead center.

Personal Journal

_____

_____

_____

_____ Date _____

DAY 311

Insight

Letting go. Letting go. Then letting go of letting go.

Reflections

When will I know? I'll never know, for the simple reason that answers and knowing are dead computer files. The second I think I know something, it is gone and becomes a memory, no longer alive and no longer truth. This is how I step out of my precious, timeless moment time after time. It is habitual, this thinking that I now know, that I have attained, and this is what's holding me back.

Meditation

Continue with forehead center concentration.

Personal Journal 🌸

_____

_____

_____

_____ *Date* _____

Part III: Insight

Concentration practice suspended our discontent and confusion by temporarily subduing thoughts and feelings, but when our concentration ended, the confusion returned, albeit in a subtly diminished capacity. The calm state of concentration only incarcerated our discontent for the moment. Before long, old habits overrode our shifts in consciousness and a jailbreak ensued, with confusion once again reigning supreme as soon as our ecstasy and calm dissipated.

Mindfulness practice went a step further, making us aware of the ignorance itself. It used our new consciousness developed from concentration practice to get at the root of our unawareness and ignorance so that they could be rehabilitated and pose no danger to us when released from their temporary prison of a concentrated mind.

Finally, insight practice will reveal the one who is unaware, the one who thinks he or she is ignorant—our "I" thought—thus eradicating the root of ignorance once and for all. But because the "I" thought keeps us alive, we shouldn't look upon it with contempt; we should understand it for what it is—innocent—in, and of, itself. It is merely "what is," or the independent arising of phenomena. Only when we lack discernment and wisdom do we allow our thoughts to build into more than independently arising phenomena. This is when they create and establish an "I" thought or self.

But why would we want to destroy this illusionary "I" thought we had to necessarily use to investigate everything during mindfulness practice? It is because if we don't, we will continually be reborn into the illusion of a self, moment to moment, and our discontent will never end.

So now we must find a way to release our "I" thought in order to acquire the freedom we seek. How do we do this? We do it by curiously doing…nothing! In a way, we stop "doing." The doer begins to break up, and as a result, the "I" thought breaks up as well. We remove the "I" thought's fuel: desire.

At some point, the witness or watcher will disappear with only pure consciousness remaining. In place of a participant, there will only be untainted observation. You can never know yourself, just as an eyeball cannot see itself, but there will be a conscious awareness apart from "you," and then, your discontent ends when your attachments to the "I" thought, and attachments to both self and no-self, are broken. At this time, a new conscious awareness will see the "I" thought, self, and no-self as separate realities, operating comfortably within the material world, innocent in, and of, themselves.

DAY 312

Insight

Like the wind, fleeting, unpredictable, without substance.

Reflections

I can never hold truth; it is far too fast and enormous for me, but can I be truth if I remain where no self exists—in the moment? If I can remain there, will my heart experience a profound, fundamental transformation, discovering the oneness of everything and the myth of individuality? My guide is here to introduce me to this beautiful, eternal moment. Why won't I listen?

Meditation

Begin with your preliminary exercises. Then divide your sessions into two parts. For the first part, proceed with your normal forehead concentration. During the second part, dwell in pure insight, where you will invite everything to enter into your open, bright mind—thoughts, emotions, feelings, everything—but hold on to nothing. Just watch it arise and pass on its own. Your mind is now a great mirror. Your mind is empty.

Personal Journal

_____

_____

_____

_____ Date _____

DAY 313

Insight

Tulips poking inquisitive heads through spring snow.

Reflections

My heart is melting. It is finally opening, and I can hear without the noises of myself.

Meditation

Continue with two-part sessions of both forehead concentration and insight practice. You are now moving into the refinement of insight, but concentration will continue to be your support. During insight practice, your object of momentary concentration will be whatever freely enters your consciousness. Open your mind and let everything and anything flow in, not choosing, rejecting, or desiring anything. Can you see a difference between concentration and insight? Concentration is a narrowing of your mind, focusing continuously on one object. Insight is an opening of your mind, a mind that has become a polished, bright mirror with no agenda and total freedom. Everything will be momentarily exposed to you before it is allowed to pass through on its own, never being held in your mind. You will be aware of every thought, but you will go far beyond this; you will get an intimate glimpse of that knower, the one beyond the watcher, the one who is aware of every thought, emotion, and feeling. You will sense the slightest movement of each thought, and the depths of every fleeting emotion. The moment of contact is the exact moment at which the contact must be allowed to pass through.

Personal Journal

_____

_____

_____

_____ _Date_ _____

DAY 314

Insight

A next step is vague unless standing in the last, a third step dubious when standing in the first.

Reflections

Why have I spent so much time concentrating on my breath? Why didn't I just start with this open awareness in the beginning?

Meditation

You must walk before you run. Necessary shifts in consciousness occur during concentration practice, therefore, concentration must be well established before tackling mindfulness and insight practice. Previously, a single object was your focus of concentration where you continually focused on the feeling of your breath. This breath is a unique concentration object and one of only a handful that leads to the mastering of concentration—other objects will not initialize deeper stages. If concentration isn't mastered first, then your mindfulness, and now your insight, will not be profound, and total liberation will be difficult. The intense concentration and mindfulness that you have developed is the only way to maintain your mind as a clear mirror during insight. With practice, you will see that there actually is no mirror, only arising and passing phenomena. Continue with your two-part sessions. Concentration must be practiced along with insight at this time.

Personal Journal

_____

_____

_____

_____ Date _____

A Year to Enlightenment

DAY 315

Insight

It lies somewhere between self and no-self.

Reflections

My mind must think...mustn't it? Of course, it must. Therefore, a delicate balance is involved here.

Meditation

Daily life requires thought; you have to get things done. But how you accomplish them now works within the context of your practice as divisive urges now give way to harmonious ones as your speech and thoughts cool. When daily life requires little thought, for example when walking or cycling, notice things but don't allow them to sustain your attention. Remain within the mindfulness and one-pointedness of concentration that you have practiced so often. They will now deepen your insight. Continue with your split sessions.

Personal Journal

_____

_____

_____

_____ _Date_ _____

DAY 316

Insight

Life's unexpected interruptions open our eyes.

Reflections

I feel as if my blinders have been removed; my vision is much sharper now. I am definitely seeing with different eyes.

Meditation

While practicing insight, notice every physical and emotional feelings of pain and joy as they arise, and let them pass through. Watch them from a place of dispassion, with no judgment against them or desire for their continuation. Allow them to enter and exit freely. Your mind and emotions are free to drift where they may, but you must be intrinsically aware of every little pull and tug the moment it occurs. Conduct no analysis, merely watch and wait, and if nothing is there, just abide in that place from which everything arises. Be completely empty. Continue with your combination of concentration and insight today.

Personal Journal

_____

_____

_____

_____ Date _____

DAY 317

Insight

Contradict everything—everything. Be empty.

Reflections

I feel myself slowly surrendering to something. I don't even know what is surrendering, or what is being surrendered to. I just know that I've never felt like this before.

Meditation

This sustained, uninterrupted, and non-discriminatory insight must be unbroken. If it isn't, you will never attain deep wisdom. Only this unrelenting, continuous awareness will bring about the penetrating insight required to reveal the no-self, or emptiness of your mental and physical processes. These things would be extremely difficult to understand if not directly experienced. How could anybody begin to know the immensity of truth without the qualities of a concentrated mind? After your preliminary exercises, spend today's sessions practicing insight, allowing everything in, and allowing it to arise and pass. You now sit in complete openness. You are only sitting, nothing more, and nothing less.

Personal Journal 🌹

_____

_____

_____

_____ Date _____

DAY 318

Insight

When we are busy memorizing what we have learned, learning stops.

Reflections

A strange feeling has come over me. How could I describe it? Never mind the concepts and practices, now there is only this calm, cool awareness. No fear is present, as if I'm sitting near a brook in a quiet forest, alone with nature and completely at peace with myself in every way. Merging with my spiritual essence has become my overriding concern.

Meditation

Spend each session today practicing forehead concentration. Concentration supports your insight practice. Always seeing things through your forehead center when out in the world will help you notice things at the exact point of contact and not let it go further into memory or thought.

Personal Journal

_____
_____
_____
_____ Date _____

DAY 319

Insight

This moment is passion. Live in it!

Reflections

Initially, I was lost and confused with my insight practice. Then, suddenly, I found myself practicing with fervor! I'm mindful day and night now, keeping my attention open wide while at the same time so inexplicably focused.

Meditation

Dedicate each session today wholly to insight. It is through insight that spirit is integrated into your heart. Remember that your insight must be uninterrupted each wakeful second of every day—yes, each wakeful second! Observe all the insights in the same manner that you notice and release images of trees while walking. Only your mindfulness together with this noticing and releasing are important now. Except for the one insight you will record in your journal each day, don't attempt to remember all the other insights or write them down. You cannot progress if you do. So much more is there to discover if you will only be patient and aloof, and maintain your discernment and equanimity. Everything discovered at this point remains mundane, not transcendent, so don't become bogged down in the mundane. The freedom you're looking for lies just beyond.

Personal Journal

_____

_____

_____

_____ Date _____

DAY 320

Insight

Suffering and pain; joining the list of great teachers.

Reflections

Life is very short. What will I do with this brief moment I call a lifetime? Saving myself for something in the future is my ongoing delusion, because when that future arrives, I will only save myself again, repeatedly, and never ultimately face the challenge. My patterns of quitting have become ingrained, saving myself endlessly and never finding enough courage to be a warrior and go beyond this self. Here is my chance to break out of this pattern of fear, this fear of emptiness, but how can I ever find my limits unless I go there? I can't stop halfway as I have done so many times in the past. For once in my life, I am going to trust. I am going to forge ahead with reckless abandonment.

Meditation

Disregard all preliminary exercises and practice pure insight today.

Personal Journal 🪷

_____

_____

_____

_____ _Date_ _____

DAY 321

Insight

Suicide is no escape.
The very same
Problems await.

Reflections

I can't leave this troublesome body until nature takes it. There are lessons still unlearned. But lately it has been so dark...and it seems to be getting worse. I feel no joy with the things of the world, nor solace with spiritual things. I am in a deep depression. However, I will persevere, no matter how long it takes. I know that there will eventually be a breakthrough, and then I will be able to help others, but until this breakthrough occurs, I can only continue my practice. There is just the painful waiting now.

Meditation

Keep your insight unbroken throughout each session today, and during your daily activities. Practice insight every waking moment until you finally meet up with your self. Seven days of unbroken insight and you will become an enlightened being.

Personal Journal

_____
_____
_____
_____ Date _____

DAY 322

Insight

Seeds are there to pick about, but not talk about.

Reflections

Why should I help humanity since they possess no self? The answer is, because humanity suffers.

Meditation

Keep your insight unbroken both day and night. Use memory and thought to function in the world, but use them sparingly. Great breakthroughs occur now, new ideas and concepts come at a rapid-fire pace. Tremendous political, social, economic, spiritual, and seemingly transcendent epiphanies will compel you to tell the world what you have discovered. Resist this. Only the weak of faith require mystery, sensationalism, and miracles; a true spiritual warrior continues his or her difficult efforts seemingly unrewarded. This is the true plight of the spiritual seeker and why humility, kindness, and self-effacement are their companions.

Personal Journal

_____

_____

_____

_____ *Date* _____

DAY 323

Insight

Learn from everything, run from nothing.

Reflections

When I began practicing this uninterrupted insight seriously, I found it difficult to relinquish control. After all, I have been controlling my life for a long time. But I did let go, little by little, aware of each impulse as it arose and then observing the arising and passing of physical emotions and mental feelings as well. I sat perfectly still while meditating, seldom moving once I settled into my position. If I had to move, I always precluded any action by noticing the impulse to act, and then I moved. I became mindful of stimulations, those initial contacts with my body or mind that preclude both physical and mental movement. I noticed each intention before each movement. This practice enabled me to see the stimulation more clearly and not be so automatic and unconscious in my responses. If my body needed to relieve itself, I first noticed the initial dull sensation and watched it slowly become stronger, then subside, then become painful again. It was just sensation, not me.

Meditation

Keep your insight intense, but this is not a battle; it is a surrender.

Personal Journal

_____

_____

_____

_____ Date _____

DAY 324

Insight

"Don't know," is a most intelligent uttering.

Reflections

I find that walking meditation challenges me to keep my mind in a state of awareness, more so than sitting meditation, and if I become very aware while walking, my sitting becomes accordingly more refined. Whenever I practice with a group, I am careful not to associate with anybody—no talking or looking around—not even a sideward glance. When I walk, it is at a slightly slower than normal, relaxed pace from one end of the path to the other with my arms hanging relaxed and my hands clasped in front, right hand over the left. With a mind silent and uncluttered, I bring my mental attention to whatever enters my consciousness, keeping my eyes two paces ahead on the path. With my mind aware and open, I know instinctively that it is extremely important not to break this moment-to-moment concentration. One peek away from this insight of walking ruins it. Sometimes if my awareness becomes intense, I will stop in the middle, or perhaps the end of the path and stand still, sometimes for long periods, before walking again.

Meditation

Spend both sessions today practicing walking meditation and working with insight.

Personal Journal

_____

_____

_____

_____ Date _____

DAY 325

Insight

Set your own pace in all things. Never fear results.

Reflections

I'm really becoming my own teacher. Even though my mind continues to struggle as my insight intensifies, and tries every diversion to free itself from these restraints, something beyond myself is helping me see, or rather helping me feel, in my heart. I keep my focus intense and remain within each moment when practicing walking meditation, just as if I was on a high wire 100 feet in the air. Doubt resurfaces and becomes severe at times, as memories and regrets attack me, but these strong doubts and hindrances merely indicate a deluded mind that is squirming under the pressure of my precise practice. I'm not about to fall prey to any beginners' mistakes by succumbing to old hindrances. If I give in now, insight will be finished.

Meditation

Practice walking meditation again, be insightful every moment without fail. Today, try to walk in natural surroundings if possible, and take a moment to appreciate the beauty of nature. Although you might not be physically able to take this beauty home, notice how your mind takes possession of it and tucks it away, to be retrieved later as enjoyable memories creating pleasurable feelings. Are you still acquiring?

Personal Journal

_____

_____

_____

_____ Date _____

DAY 326

Insight

From atoms to universes, where can consciousness not be found?

Reflections

I simply watch my doubts and memories without adding anything to them. They arise, and there is no problem with that. Problems only crop up when I forget that these doubts and memories are merely arising and passing occurrences that I mistakenly identify as reality. Then they have power over me. So now I just observe them without judging, knowing that every thought in meditation, as well as every experience in life, will soon be on its way.

Meditation

Continue with your walking meditation and insight practice. When we are able to truly see something, even for only a moment, that is the end of it. If we can see how we continue acquiring things, such as memories, insights, and ideas, and how we hang on to them, unwilling to let them slip away, unwilling to admit their unimportance, then we can realize what keeps us in the mundane. However, the moment we see this process within ourselves, it is the beginning of the end of that particular illusion, even though its manifestations will persist— for a long time.

Personal Journal

_____

_____

_____

_____ *Date* _____

A Year to Enlightenment

DAY 327

Insight

If it expands you, beware. If it diminishes you, continue.

Reflections

I become very creative during meditation. My consciousness expands and out pops great ideas. But I can't allow myself to be misled by these immense conclusions and incredible illuminations. My progress could be delayed for years if I stop and examine every newfound insight. Permanent liberation is far more important to me than this preliminary wisdom because I want to help the human race, but how can I effectively do that if my practice isn't fully developed? I would end up blind, trying to lead the blind, and things wouldn't change. War, greed, starving children, and little concern for the sick, the poor and the old, those without voices, would continue to be the results of unenlightened thought.

Meditation

Resume sitting meditation and insight practice. Now you're just watching, not actively investigating. This is very easy; just watch everything come and go. Once you place yourself under the restraint of this insight, you will no longer analyze things. Just practice and see the results for yourself.

Personal Journal 🪷

_____

_____

_____

_____ _Date_ _____

DAY 328

Insight

I know not where or when or how
This life continuum will pass
Eternal is the moment now
My providence to the winds I cast.

Reflections

I find myself moving here, traveling there, always following my heart and intuition. And no matter how persuasive my logic and reason are in trying to dissuade me, I somehow carry on. Meditation exposes me to direct insight and wisdom, but I must be cautious. Logic and reason persistently attempt to capture and control these direct insights by building permanent beliefs within me, abducting me from the spontaneity of each moment, and imprisoning me in the lifeless pit of knowledge. I must guard against this danger, for it is most insidious. It will stop me dead in my tracks if I am seduced into spending all of my energy constructing a false spiritual empire built upon the unstable sands of self. Then I will be cursed with merely the ashes of truth, filled with self-righteous opinions and arguments that have precipitated humanity's greatest conflicts. Far removed will I find myself, not only from this precious moment, but from my spiritual essence and greater insights as well.

Meditation

Continue with insight practice. Be careful of establishing images or concepts about it. It must always be moment to moment.

Personal Journal

_____
_____
_____
_____ Date _____

DAY 329

Insight

For being arises like a phoenix
With wings outstretched and hungry eyes
And then becoming follows after
And oceans fill with tears we cry.

Reflections

I have ambitiously pursued enlightenment. Has this become a road of desire for me? Has it led to further competitiveness within myself as I struggle to become something I feel that I'm not? As long as I seek, I will always be in this state of becoming, becoming something, strongly wanting something, wanting more and more, but when I no longer seek and the road is merely traveled because it is there, what will happen? Will the destination, as well as the journey, turn into love? Perhaps only then can I relax into my moment of eternity.

Meditation

Remain secure within your insight. Stay within each moment as it arises. Eventually, there will be but one long, continuous moment, timeless, and stretching into eternity. Your eyes must open slowly during this moment so the shock is bearable, for arriving at a place where experience ends is harrowing for the inexperienced traveler—a traveler who is still on the road and has yet to see the emptiness of all things. Some questions might never be answered, but soon, no answers will be needed.

Personal Journal

_____
_____
_____
_____ Date _____

DAY 330

Insight

Become as nothing and everything will come.

Reflections

As my search continues, I find myself being called stupid and useless, and scorned by people of every walk of life. Many do not understand this extraordinary struggle. I'll not inform those that ridicule, particularly ones who think their way is the only way, for they are the most fearful and will only become angry. They will call me rude and strange, and decide if I am perceived to be a threat to their beliefs. They might possibly want to kill me. Others, who are more tolerant, will merely laugh at me as an ignorant fool. There are those, however, whose eyes are closed but slightly and are almost ready to see. They are the ones who will understand.

Meditation

As you continue practicing insight, you will eventually develop a detached overview, something you have never had. Nobody will be home, and this will instill wisdom. This wisdom, in turn, will alter your thought patterns, and then your altered thought patterns will create additional wisdom, as everything begins cycling in the direction of your spiritual essence. Your "I" thought will dissolve completely and when this happens, you will be afraid, but for only a brief moment during that vacuum when your "I" thought vanishes and your spiritual essence appears. Your spirit has always been right here, in your heart, but forever suppressed by your root of desire and attachment to your small self, and as you slowly leave your familiar world behind, you must develop the wisdom to somehow remain in it.

Personal Journal

_____

_____

_____

_____ _Date_ _____

DAY 331

Insight

Soft velvet ribbons that bind like iron chains around our necks.

Reflections

One day, I realized how I use my dearest friends and family as merely mutual stimulations, playthings for my physical senses. One would think that a callous feeling would result from this kind of experience, but that was not the case at all. On the contrary, when the insight occurred there was an unburdening—a feeling in my heart of liberation and an authentic, unconditional love that washed over the previous feelings of unhealthy manipulation, clinging, and possessiveness. This unconditional love is difficult to describe. It isn't the love that researchers can create by artificially stimulating portions of the brain. This transcends that kind of experience. But love is the closest I can come to describing it, even though that description is woefully inadequate. Delight is still present, even stronger, but no longer distorted by attachment. It is a free joy, an all-encompassing love, a true affection no longer dependent on mutual security. Everybody is seen as delightful emanations of love, without my need to claim ownership or fear their loss.

Meditation

Remain thoroughly involved with this undirected insight, inviting everything in but clinging to nothing. Let even the one who is reflecting everything back dissolve, so that there is no longer any doer, just bare consciousness.

Personal Journal

_____
_____
_____
_____ _Date_ _____

7 Attributes of Enlightenment

What are the attributes of enlightened beings? Surely, such beings would be extremely mindful and curious, investigating everything with an unlimited energy and also rapture that would accompany their endeavors, yet with an underlying tranquility. They certainly would have an extraordinary ability to concentrate their minds and they would be filled with equanimity as well. Of these seven things, you may be certain.

DAY 332

Insight

Love is always there, smothered by concern.

Reflections

Meditation seems to involve no beliefs. It is a constant discovery, and once that discovery is made, once the insight arises, I know the results in my heart to be true. I know when I'm being mindful, when I'm rapturous, when I'm keen to investigate things, and I know when I have unlimited energy. I am aware when I am tranquil, and when I am concentrating my mind, and when I experience equanimity.

Meditation

Disregard the idea that you are not enlightened. Carefully watch who or what it is that worries about enlightenment. Watch carefully the one who meditates and the one who is striving. Get to know the "I" thought intimately through self-inquiry. Watch the "I" thought night and day. The "I" thought is you; it is your emotions and feelings, it is your thoughts, your mind. Cling to this "I" thought at all times to discover its make-up. As long as you are completely aware of it, no other thoughts can intervene. As in beginning meditation, you will need to reject other thoughts as you focus on this "I" thought, but in time, what lies underneath this "I" thought reveals itself, and what is revealed is the one who knows but is not involved. At some point, you will no longer have to struggle to keep stray thoughts at bay. It will happen automatically. There will no longer be any kind of struggle. Strife will be impossible as your life becomes trouble-free and effortless.

Personal Journal 🪷

_____

_____

_____

_____ Date _____

DAY 333

Insight

Mindfulness—always alert, with vigorous anticipation.

Reflections

I must let everything go. I must stay within my insight always.

Meditation

Mindfulness, the first aspect of enlightenment, is central to seeing clearly. It reflects a non-selective, willing awareness filled with openness, freedom, and the authentic virtue of dispassion. Use it now to self-inquire into your "I" thought every moment. This is not difficult because with the exception of when thoughts are absent, your "I" thought is right in front of you at all times. Don't separate yourself from your "I" thought, don't fight against it, don't think about it, just be it completely, so completely that there is no room left for any other thoughts to intervene. Watch the "I" thought, watch the watcher constantly, until both the "I" thought and the watcher disappear. They are both merely thoughts, merely mind. The mind is a tool to get us by in this physical world, but there is no you getting by, no mind getting by. However, there is an underlying reality which is conscious of the "I" thought. It is the detached observer, the one that is choicelessly aware, the uncreated, unborn, and undying. It is beyond mind, beyond the watcher, and beyond the "I" thought. It is a knowing that can be experienced...and the experience of this knowing will radically change your destiny.

Personal Journal

_____

_____

_____

_____ Date _____

DAY 334

Insight

A curious seeing exists, but you can't see it.

Reflections

Investigation or insight is the second aspect, and defines the relationship between my illusions. It helps me see that nobody is actually there to do the observing, that I am simply what I observe. Only this powerful mindfulness can free me from the concept of my small self.

Meditation

You are not limited to your body and mind, and the moment you really see this, your body and mind will automatically fall away, as something else reveals itself. Watch your "I" thought carefully, asking, Who am I? Or What am I? This does not involve a struggle of any kind. Just watch yourself closely, excluding everything else. This watching is only memory at this point, but eventually that something will arise, that which is beyond both "I" thought and watcher. Then freedom begins.

Personal Journal

_____

_____

_____

_____ *Date* _____

DAY 335

Insight

Embark on a vivid, dynamic life of understanding.

Reflections

The third aspect, energy, develops involuntarily when my mind is completely absorbed with something of great interest. When mindfulness of both my inside world and my outside world really takes hold, energy is limitless.

Meditation

Watch your "I" thought relentlessly now—at work, at play, when resting, when meditating. With your extensive experience of going within, it will be easy to do. The "I" thought will frequently show up as a picture in your mind—as yourself—a picture of your face or body, or you might find yourself talking to yourself. It is there almost constantly—you can't miss it. All you have to do is watch it, keeping all other thoughts away. By watching the "I" thought continuously, the "I" thought cannot interact with other objects and it eventually disappears, and so do you.

Personal Journal

_____

_____

_____

_____ *Date* _____

DAY 336

Insight

At times, a heart can barely stand the overwhelming ecstasy.

Reflections

Passion or rapture, the fourth aspect, is unavoidable when my everyday mind is transcended—even for a brief moment. The resulting feeling of relief can only be described as unimaginable, unbridled liberation.

Meditation

Mind, which creates your "I" thought, is derived from your spiritual essence, but your spiritual essence is not your mind. When your mind turns within, it turns toward your spiritual essence, but when it turns outwardly, it becomes your "I" thought, and turns toward the world. Keep the mind focused inwardly on itself. Remain focused on your small self, your "I" thought, constantly now.

Personal Journal 🌹

_____

_____

_____

_____ Date _____

DAY 337

Insight

Tranquility is rare, confusion commonplace.

Reflections

I find that tranquility, the fifth aspect of enlightenment, is not daydreaming or a trance state. It is a precise understanding that nothing is important on one level, yet on another, each moment is everything.

Meditation

Laugh, play, be involved with everything now, but never lose sight of your "I" thought, not for one moment. Don't attempt to alter it or change it; don't attempt to gain enlightenment or anything of that nature. You are observing your "I" thought, and that is all that is to be done. Any attempted action would involve your "I" thought at this stage and that would only strengthen the illusion. You needn't even look for the "I" thought, for it is always right there. Just be aware of it.

Personal Journal

_____
_____
_____
_____ _Date_ _____

DAY 338

Insight

Circling, circling, swooping low, then higher.

Reflections

The sixth aspect is concentration—the necessary key in order to penetrate spiritual truths. Some who are born enlightened insist that I forget about concentration, assuming that I have the ability to see clearly and immediately without effort, as they can, but knots don't untangle that easily for everyday people like me. The knots were created by my confused mind, then increasingly tightened by that mind, and only going beyond this mind can untangle them. Once the knots are loosened, only then does the possibility exist to transcend this mind. I can't pull myself out of a hole without a rope, so what good is it, at this point, for someone to walk up and say, "Be enlightened?" An untrained mind would surely laugh at the notion.

Meditation

Your "I" thought is a subject. Concentration, mindfulness, and insight practice have enabled you to see this "I" thought easily and clearly now, but since any meditation or practice must involve effort and a subject and object, the "I" thought remains strong. Your essence requires no subject or object and can only be experienced directly, so when your "I" thought is seen through; all that will be left is your spiritual essence that has been covered up by it. Keep watching that "I" thought until it dissolves by itself into your essence.

Personal Journal 🌸

_____

_____

_____

_____ *Date* _____

DAY 339

Insight

The woman once foolishly considered herself a saint. Now she has eyes of wisdom.

Reflections

The final aspect of enlightenment is equanimity. Equanimity sees all things with equal eyes. It differentiates but doesn't evaluate. It is a dispassion of great passion, it is composure, and it is an unbridled evenness going far beyond normal action and reaction.

Meditation

When watching your "I" thought, secondary thoughts have difficulty arising. There will only be that one "I" thought in front of you. Stay with the "I" thought, for when you don't, other thoughts return vigorously. You must tear the heart out of all thoughts completely, including the "I" thought, and this requires abandoning effort at some point and experiencing your spiritual essence. More than that, it involves being your spiritual essence.

Personal Journal

_____

_____

_____

_____ Date _____

DAY 340

Insight

Toiling for no reward awakens wisdom.

Reflections

My practice is an unselfish endeavor. When I study my own mind, I'm really studying everybody's mind. My greed, my dislike for others, and my misunderstanding of the truth are no different from your experiences. Therefore, it is not I who practices for myself, it is humankind that practices.

Meditation

It is not a matter of effort. In the beginning, it might seem like an effort to just be whatever you are, but after a while, it will all be effortless. At some point the "I" thought will cease to exist, and then what emerges is your true spiritual essence. This could be a sudden but not usually a permanent change at first, there will be some backsliding, but as you persist in being what you are, eventually the "I" thought will be gone forever. Until that time arrives, however, be that "I" thought completely.

Personal Journal 🌹

_____

_____

_____

_____ Date _____

DAY 341

Insight

Sipping tea at night; frogs rejoicing.

Reflections

My life is filled with many things. Can I maintain this normal lifestyle while living each moment freely, unburdening myself, yet still live in the world? I think that this is not only possible, but perhaps the only hope of humankind's continued existence. Is this the next level of human consciousness?

Meditation

Meditation has taught you about your mind. Now, remain with the mind, don't fight it any longer. Be your "I" thought completely until you have seen through it so thoroughly that the mystery is gone. It is only thoughts and feelings, and when they disappear, there before you is your spiritual essence. But if the thought ever occurs that you have realized your essence, then of course, you have not. This would be a backsliding into discursive thinking. Realization can only take place in this one, precious moment, and only when the moments string together, is there enlightenment.

Personal Journal

_____
_____
_____
_____ Date _____

DAY 342

Insight

Quietness eases across the evening, the constant stars console me.

Reflections

A time will come when speculating stops. I will suddenly throw everything out, my thoughts and whatever else there is, and let it my spirit take me.

Meditation

No more exercises, no more concentration, no more mindfulness. You are now just being either your "I" thought or your essence. What matters is that you are being what you are, not what you think you are, or what you want to be, and that you realize, every moment of every waking hour, what exactly it is that you are.

Personal Journal

_____
_____
_____
_____ *Date* _____

DAY 343

Insight

Emptiness must be plumbed before its fullness is known.

Reflections

When I consider emptiness, it is only my ideas of emptiness. There will be that moment, however, when I am emptiness. Then I'll know. And on that day, my fear will be vanquished forever.

Meditation

Doing nothing, only sitting quietly now waiting for It to infuse you. This is thinking beyond thinking, thinking beyond non-thinking. Now there is no goal for enlightenment, no wish to change yourself or gain anything. Following no techniques, you sit in quiet anticipation.

Personal Journal 🪷

_____
_____
_____
_____ D_{ate} _____

DAY 344

Insight

Absence defines a material void; fullness, an immaterial void; and creation, voids beyond.

Reflections

I must remain steadfast. I mustn't allow my preoccupied mind to hold me endlessly as a prisoner in the past and future. I can't let it steal this precious moment that is my legacy, my true being of unbridled freedom and love. I see instinctively that this moment is completely alive, unknown, and immeasurable, embracing enlightenment. It surely must be timeless and as vast as eternity, reflecting my true beginnings, the only place I could truly be defined. Finally, when I'm able to step into the moment and remain there, I trust that my entire being will be transformed, moved supernaturally from selfish fear into all-encompassing love. Then I'll know, without knowing, that everything is perfect, just as it is.

Meditation

True meditation is seeing through this "I" thought by the process of being your "I" thought until it understands itself, liberating the mind and all of its illusions.

Personal Journal

_____
_____
_____
_____ Date _____

DAY 345

Insight

Will you tie a boat to your back once the voyage is over?

Reflections

I will never find truth. I can only sort through the false—but when the false is revealed, will truth then find me? If so, then I will no longer be required to search for it. I will become it. I have had extraordinary experiences, each being a milestone in my epic journey, but like dissipating fog, a remaining patch of delusion lingers here and there. I try to blow the fog away, but to no avail; it will only vanish in time. Patience is again required.

Meditation

Once you see through this "I" thought, you will become your essence, free to dive into the world without being affected. Things will occur but there will be no enduring impact. There will only be the next moment, then the next, and the next. There will be doing, but no longer a doer.

Personal Journal

_____

_____

_____

_____ Date _____

DAY 346

Insight

Nothing matters.

Reflections

I have experienced wisdom in my practice, but that wisdom is dead and gone. Any attempt to resurrect it and apply it to this new moment is folly. Surely, wisdom must be a potential, never a possession, for truth can only be found here, right in this very moment. Instead of being proud of my wisdom, I will surrender it and remain in constant awareness in which far greater truths await.

Meditation

Permanent and non-stop conscious awareness of your spiritual essence is felt as bliss. But it is not known to any "I" thought. The mind and the "I" thought cannot exist here. There is only direct action because of this infinite awareness.

Personal Journal

_____

_____

_____

_____ _Date_ _____

DAY 347

Insight

Quickly, surrender emptiness and the moment. Where are you?

Reflections

It is always a relinquishing. I spend so much energy building it up and then even more energy destroying it. Can I ever stop building? The key is the builder.

Meditation

Everything that is done is now done for others.

Personal Journal

_____
_____
_____
_____ *Date* _____

DAY 348

Insight

I have traveled over vast waters and beyond great mountains. The moon is the same.

Reflections

Can I remain in the moment? It is very simple. I just need to do it! This moment is right here. Nowhere else must I travel to find it. It has always been right here, within reach, but because I could never see this, I insisted on taking the long path, discovering what was holding me back. I had to investigate my entire consciousness with my discriminating and focused intelligence. First, I learned to concentrate, and then I used those resulting shifts in consciousness to investigate every facet of my body and mind. But one thing persisted, one thing held me back from experiencing this eternal moment—my lack of insight into the truth that there is no self. I have studied the self for a long time now—isn't it time to release it, let it go, let everything go. This is the only way I will ever attain insight. It took a long time, but now I understand the price of enlightenment; it is everything. This is why I need my guide; I can't let go of myself—by myself—not quite yet.

Meditation

The "I" thought is now gone. No longer is it necessary for a thinker to think. There are only thoughts arising within a vast field of consciousness.

Personal Journal

_____

_____

_____

_____ Date _____

DAY 349

Insight

Once you realize it, you will live it.

Reflections

Bound to my senses, I still enjoy everything in the world, but the enjoyment is from a different, unrestricted viewpoint now. Everything is reflected back into its own beauty instead of being lodged in my mind as desire, which awakens possession, which awakens violence. Think how much more delightful every moment of life would be without the burden of owning it. How could I hope for a quiet mind, absent of discontent, while still engaged in wanting and grasping?

Meditation

No effort is needed now. You no longer require being anything, only being. The doing is done, being has begun.

Personal Journal

_____

_____

_____

_____ Date _____

DAY 350

Insight

I drift through my days.

Reflections

I am unquestionably approaching the ultimate simplification through meditation. As I practice, I notice necessary decisions naturally becoming straightforward. I can envision this simplicity rising in an upward spiral, ultimately coming to a single point where I can remain in each moment without distraction. I have an opportunity to reach that single point with my meditation, but only by daring effort can I resist hiding behind this false image of my self and go beyond it. If I am ready to take this risk, my guide has offered to direct me toward unfamiliar waters.

Meditation

A meditator, meditation, or a meditation object is no longer remembered. It all arises in a field of silence now. This consciousness is your new identity. Your old body and mind are gone.

Personal Journal

_____

_____

_____

_____ *Date* _____

DAY 351

Insight

Who becomes enlightened?

Reflections

I feel released, like a reprieve from a terminal illness. Perhaps, in a way, this is precisely true.

Meditation

No meditator, no meditation, no journey, everything is gone. There is something new now; it has nothing to do with you, and still...it is all of you.

Personal Journal

_____

_____

_____

_____ _Date_ _____

DAY 352

Insight

When it happens, you will know it.

Reflections

Will I retire to a cave once I'm enlightened? Probably not, but life will unquestionably be experienced from a different point of view. Meditation, which in the beginning involved great effort to keep out intruding thoughts, will now become constant and effortless—a natural state of perfect existence. Thought, when necessary, only will arise out of indescribable emptiness, and my previous battles to be free of what flowed into my senses will no longer be necessary, just as a man who has quenched his thirst forever stops searching for water. The pressing need to achieve things will be gone, because everything will have been done. No more struggling to become anything—other than what I am, accepting everything, rejecting nothing. Only unconditional, undirected attention of the independent arisings that come into the fields of my body and mind will now be my life—a mirror with everything reflected. My mind will no longer grasp anything. The big "I," the self, will be gone. No longer will I find myself striving to become something that I'm not. Ambition and struggling will cease, with no agendas, no fears, just maintaining my last body, my last human form. The goal of goallessness is near.

Meditation

Now an effortless way of life.

Personal Journal

_____

_____

_____

_____ Date _____

DAY 353

Insight

Meditation is but a fuse, slowly burning toward understanding...Boom!

Reflections

It is difficult to continue with practice now. I find myself moved to help others, or perhaps write a book and share my understanding. I have free will and may do as I choose, but something tells me not to hurry. My understanding is not complete. I'm sure that my progress will end as soon as practice stops. Someday, my spiritual essence will utilize my natural talents to increase the consciousness of humankind. Then I might very well be a great help, but not yet. My self is still involved.

Meditation

Just the moment exists now, where insight is never ending. Everything evolves; nothing is static. Your books and your teachings are dead, even before they are written or spoken. Let it all go now—all the insights, all the wondrous experiences and explanations of how the universe works; it is all acquisitions. Let them go. Don't worry about recording it for posterity. Just be.

Personal Journal

_____

_____

_____

_____ Date _____

DAY 354

Insight

Crickets on a warm summer's night, a hand held as a last breath is taken. Exquisite.

Reflections

Until I let go of my self, my "I" thought will cling to me like sweat, following me into the after-world and affecting my every existence. To go beyond what I am now, I must go beyond what I now am. The house is demolished. Why do I continue to sleep with my tools?

Meditation

Stillness. Things unmoving. Great silence crescendos into shafts of light.

Personal Journal

_____
_____
_____
_____ $\mathcal{D}_{ate}$ _____

Enlightenment Experiences

If you could taste a color, how would you describe it? Or if you could experience infinity for one brief moment—how would you begin to explain it? We talk in images that are admittedly inaccurate, but that's the best we can do; that's the limit of mundane human understanding. Enlightenment is love, a unique, ineffable love that cannot be defined, cannot be explained, and far removed from what we believe love to be.

DAY 355

Insight

When you can't grasp it, you are making progress.

Reflections

Am "I" in the moment? No, there is just that. The idea that I am in the moment with something else is an illusion. No room exists for both the apparition—me, and that, which is truly present. It therefore follows that "I" must be that! The moment must be all of me. I am that. The implications of this are enormous: If there is loneliness, loneliness is that. It is the truth; it is the reality of that precise moment…and it is me! It is not something happening to me, or something that I can control or wish away in that exact moment; it is there. But it is not me who is lonely; there is only loneliness, with nothing standing behind it. It is there, I am that, but it's only there for one moment, quickly disappearing into the next with only a memory keeping the image alive. Once this understanding drops into my heart, how could I ever be lonely again? How could I ever again be in conflict with myself? Could I finally be whole?

Meditation

Your understanding and your progress on this journey are as nothing while you now sit in the silence of the cosmos. Nobody is here—an empty cushion.

Personal Journal

_____

_____

_____

_____ *Date* _____

DAY 356

Insight

All-encompassing love grows in the rich soil of understanding.

Reflections

With the fog slowly clearing, love unexpectedly surrounds me, and the love is real, it is the truth, it is what is here in the moment. It is unlike anything I have ever experienced. I am the love; it is not happening to me. It is me. I am that, I am love, I am nothing else, for there is nothing standing behind the love. How perfect.

Meditation

No sound, no thought, no Earth, no other world, only...this—right here.

Personal Journal

_____
_____
_____
_____ *Date* _____

Insight

A universe within each drop.

Reflections

Suddenly, I find myself appearing in the middle of a great circle in the center of space, and I feel as if a flood is carrying me to the edge of a void. My concentration on this image is intense. I can feel it, I touch it, and in the next instant, I, as well as the center of the circle vanish in a flash, with only the circumference of the circle remaining.

Meditation

Just sitting now. The moonlight, your solitary friend, drifts through your window as you sit like a mountain bathed in white light...still, serene.

Personal Journal

_____

_____

_____

_____ _Date_ _____

DAY 358

Insight

Experiencing now ends.

Reflections

This circumference immediately begins to expand, larger and larger, until it swallows the entire universe. It continues to increase, engulfing all knowledge and all perception, going beyond all worlds, beyond everything known and everything unknown. I plummet into each stage of concentration, one after the other in rapid succession. The primal energy, sitting at the base of my spine, begins its upward movement, faster and faster, spinning through the other six centers, whirling round and round, as my body, then my mind with its contact, feeling, memory, and imagination, all shatter like thin glass as a million suns suddenly flash. I finally know there was never anyone searching and there was never a search, there was only this...this inexpressible something, all along.

Meditation

No further questions, no more mysteries. Who is still present to question? Of what use is the knowledge of answers?

Personal Journal

_____

_____

_____

_____ Date _____

DAY 359

Insight

A crescendo of light.

Reflections

I am leaping with great fear, yet with great courage, into an immense vacuum of white nothingness, and from this white nothingness arises everything. I am accelerating beyond the third dimension, into the fourth and then the fifth, the sixth, the seventh and then beyond every conceivable dimension. I see every form and non-form, spheres and time and universes, contracting and expanding in great breaths, countless universes, each beginning from nothing and spraying out endlessly before dissolving, and within this immensity, I see other beginnings, as there are no endings, only constant movement.

Meditation

Now, let your meditation take you wherever it may, with no further attachment or relationship to anything in the universe.

Personal Journal

_____

_____

_____

_____ *Date* _____

DAY 360

Insight

And the goddesses danced and danced.

Reflections

I find myself strangely free from circumstances, with no previous regrets or future agendas, immersed in the universal consciousness of every being since the beginning of beginningless time. I come face to face with the Source of all things, and in this seeing realize that the Source is all of me, and I fall completely into its arms, as the moment and everything in it...ends.

Meditation

And the effort is now gone. Only This remains.

Personal Journal

_____

_____

_____

_____ Date _____

DAY 361

Insight

The seasons patter on my gray head like rain on a tin roof.

Reflections

I have never before seen life in this manner, this harmony, this ordinary cycle of things, unhurried and calm, confident and sure with nothing out of place and nothing needed. It is as if, for the first time, I can really see without the heavy veil of myself clouding the way. How beautiful it all is. How natural...

Meditation

Everything is perfect; it just happens.

Personal Journal

_____
_____
_____
_____ *Date* _____

DAY 362

Insight

The clouds have passed. The moon...so brilliant.

Reflections

The spiritual nature of the world is opening before my very eyes. I am immersed in the discovery that I am inseparable from the world and everything in it—it is all merely reflections of the great Source within me. All-encompassing love is everywhere and nothing truly matters now, as I merge with my spiritual essence, a unity that is indescribable.

Meditation

Stillness; the exquisite silence of the stars.

Personal Journal

_____

_____

_____

_____ Date _____

A Year to Enlightenment

DAY 363

Insight

A beacon to humankind, her light blankets the Earth with compassion and wisdom.

Reflections

The world is now an expression of the love I have become. The Source is not only inside of me but surrounds me, everywhere; it infuses me. I am that Source...but I'm not, for it is like a great, burning star that will sear me if I venture too close, and yet I know that I will perish if I stray too far away. I am overflowing with its emptiness, the fullest emptiness in all the worlds. Suddenly, I find myself filled with something much greater. This is beyond any insight I could have ever imagined. Incredibly, I comprehend the cessation of my own existence. The flame has gone out.

Meditation

Experience nears its end; there just is that. There is nothing left to do. Now you are free, free from everything. You are finally home.

Personal Journal

_____

_____

_____

_____ _Date_ _____

DAY 364

Insight

Drifting down the river, my paddle long lost.

Reflections

Comfortable with what I am now; easy, unhurried, confident. No matter what happens, I have my understanding. Not too many wants any more, I need little to eat and can live anywhere. I have a freedom, but not a freedom that depends on the satisfaction of desires, for each of those satisfactions breeds more desires. I have a far greater freedom; I am nothing.

Meditation

Nowhere to go now, having come from nowhere.

Personal Journal

_____
_____
_____
_____ Date _____

DAY 365

Insight

I sleep on the ground, my high bed abandoned.

Reflections

I have little to say now, only a smile. You have met people like me, but probably don't remember them. I like it that way, not even burdening you with memories.

Meditation

Your guide will be forever with you.

Personal Journal

_____
_____
_____
_____ *Date* _____

About the Author

E. Raymond Rock of Fort Myers, Florida, is cofounder and principal teacher at Southwest Florida Insight Center (*www.southwestfloridainsightcenter.com*). His 27 years of meditation experience have taken him across four continents, including two stopovers in Thailand where he practiced in the remote northeast forests as an ordained Theravada Buddhist monk. He lived at Wat Pah Nanachat under the beloved teacher Ajahn Chah; and at Wat Pah Baan Taad under Ajahn Maha Boowa, currently the most venerated forest meditation monk in Thailand.

He has been a postulant at Shasta Abbey, a Zen Buddhist monastery in northern California under Roshi Kennett; and a Theravada Buddhist anagarika at both Amaravati Monastery in the UK and Bodhinyanarama Monastery in New Zealand, both under Ajahn Sumedho.

The author has meditated with the world-renowned Sri Lankan monk, Bhante Gunaratana at the Bhavana Society in West Virginia, as well as the Korean Master Sun Sunim; and with Tibetan Master Trungpa Rinpoche in Boulder, Colorado. He has also practiced at the Insight Meditation Society in Barre, Massachusetts, and at the Zen Center in San Francisco.